WILDSAM

What a chatter the birds set up
When the sun broke out on the trembling air,
We flung off our caps and the little red pigs
Were beside themselves and ran everywhere.

—*James Hearst, "Blue Again"*

WILDSAM PURSUITS

Places are endlessly complex: time, geography, culture and happenings layered with millions of stories. And often, one realizes that a place carries a specific heritage, a definitive pursuit that people build their lives around, a common trade or precious resource that might set the course for generations.

For Iowa, this pursuit is writing.

This book comes of graceful moments of aid. In particular, Jane Van Voorhis revealed many Iowa splendors and opened many doors; Christopher Brewer stuck with us through every twist and turn. The University of Iowa is lucky to have both. Our guides were many: Hannah and Thomas Agran, Danny Khalastchi, Lila Byock, Jordan Sellergren, Andre Perry and Andres at Bartender's Handshake. Sasha Khmelnik, Ethan Canin, Raeden Richardson, Drew Bratcher and others brought us into Iowa City. Carolyn Swayze realized our diamond dreams.

WILDSAM FIELD GUIDES™

Published in the United States
by Wildsam Field Guides, Austin, Texas.
"Shoeless Joe Jackson Comes to Iowa" appears courtesy the W.P. Kinsella Estate. The description of Marilynne Robinson's class on *Moby-Dick* appears courtesy Drew Bratcher.

ISBN 978-1-4671-9978-0

Illustrations by Ananda Walden

To find more field guides, please visit
www.wildsam.com

CONTENTS

Discover the people and places
that tell the story of the Iowa Prairie

WELCOME

THE NOVELIST JOSEPHINE DONOVAN grew up in Granville, a farm town northeast of Sioux City. Her 1930 book *The Black Soil* told some of that wide country's story, a tale of immigrant farmers drifting out across Iowa's ocean of land, looking to get roots in the ground. She has a line that still feels right almost a century later: "The prairie stretched to the end of the world." Even now, that is how it feels when you're out in the heart of Iowa, where fields and woods go on and on. So, too, does Iowa's roll call of writers, artists and thinkers like Josephine Donovan, moved to create here. The Iowa soil runs deep in more ways than one.

As we traveled the state, we met many proud Iowans, and they told us many more true, useful things about their place. Another line that stuck: "Iowa will surprise you."

Stereotype tells of a flat country; the map depicts tidy grids of farm roads and long, straight highways. None of that captures the real feeling. The landscape rolls and undulates to its own surfy rhythm. Water towers mark towns long before the lines of buildings crest the horizon. In those towns—who knows? Maybe a small but beautiful art museum. A feisty little newspaper that fights the good fight. A throwback bar with a statewide cult following. The best bagel in a long time. Iowa will surprise you.

The original tallgrass prairie that Donovan wrote about is almost all gone, sacrificed for agriculture. But it's not *quite* gone. Swatches of reedy grasses and wildflowers survive, here and there. From the outside, depending on the season, prairie can look monochrome. Wander into it, and layers and textures reveal themselves. Today, many Iowans are working to bring prairie back, with painstaking planting, controlled burns, even a precious few bison ambling on the horizon. What folks find: when the prairie comes back, life comes back, in delirious diversity—bugs, birds, roots that rebuild that black soil. At best, a state that does a lot to feed the world discovers new ways to take care of itself.

Across history, Iowans have tallied up a lot of accomplishments. Founded the world's first advanced school for poets and novelists. Out-wrestled all comers. Invented new ways to till fields and harvest crops. Hit the grooves that defined hot jazz. The larger point is, Iowans get things done. Together, they've created a land to explore. —The Editors

SELECTED CONTENT

Trusted intel and travel info about iconic culture, geography and entry points to the traditions and landscapes of Iowa and the prairie country

PLANNING

TRANSPORT

PADDLEBOAT
Riverboat *Twilight*
LeClair to Dubuque
riverboattwilight.com

BICYCLES
Iowa City Bike Library
Iowa City
@bikelibrarian

LANDMARKS

HAMBURG INN NO. 2
Iowa City
Longtime campaign stop, home of the Coffee Bean Caucus.

SOLDIERS' AND SAILORS' MONUMENT
Des Moines
Towering memorial obelisk flanked by some *florid* statuary.

MEDIA

CITY PAPER
Des Moines Register
Historic statewide titan, with national-scope politics coverage.

TOWN PAPER
Storm Lake Times-Pilot
Family-run semiweekly takes on big ag. Pulitzer winner in 2017.

LITERARY JOURNAL
Brink
Crossing genres with hybrid forms.

CLIMATE

The Iowa year is a long cycle of extremes and sweet spots. Pick a starting point: maybe April, time of bunnies and dogwood, serviceberry, morels, prairie grasses and prairie flowers, earth-giant thunderstorms. In May, plant things; they'll grow. Summer means humidity, commented upon at county fairs, best survived via long bike rides. After autumn's harvest season, November brings cool times but also some outlier perfect, windless weeks. Winter's frozen faces and short days call for cross-country skis and thick new novels.

CALENDAR

J/F	Iowa caucuses [quadrennial]
FEB	High school wrestling finals, Des Moines
MAR	Oneota Film Festival, Decorah
APR	Morel mushroom picking
MAY	Writers' Workshop theses
JUN	TrekFest, Riverside
JUL	RAGBRAI bike tour
AUG	Iowa State Fair
SEP	Fort Madison Mexican Fiesta
OCT	World Food Prize
NOV	Farm Toy Show, Dyersville
DEC	Brucemore Mansion Christmas, Cedar Rapids

GEOGRAPHY

Notable terrain formations and where to find them.

DRIFTLESS AREA
Untouched by Ice Age glaciers, the state's northeast corner is slashed with limestone bluffs and winding river byways. *Yellow River State Forest*

TALLGRASS PRAIRIE
The Iowa biome, now rare but astonishing. Home to dense insect, plant, bird and mammal life. *Tallgrass Prairie Center, Cedar Falls*

TAMA SOIL
In a state defined by its fertility, this is the mascot soil. Formed by prairie grass and humidity, now endangered by erosion. *Black Hawk County*

FOSSIL GORGE
Big floods just 30 years ago revealed ancient Devonian period sea floor and bountiful fossils. *Iowa City*

KETTLEHOLES
Depressions left by giant blocks of melting ice, eons ago. Refuge for rare plants. *Freda Haffner Preserve*

LOESS SOILS
River silt built into hills by westerly winds. Razor ridges, cat-step terraces. *Sawmill Hollow Wildlife Area*

TRADITIONS

A state defined by creativity, cultivation and a certain kind of grit.

Writing — The University of Iowa's Writers' Workshop helps orchestrate national literary culture. Programs at Grinnell and Iowa State shine too. *Dog-Eared Books, Ames*

Wrestling — Raucous crowds in the thousands and a long roster of champs make Iowa the grapplers' true heartland. *Dan Gable Museum, Waterloo*

Pork — In the top hog state, it's an economic staple and culinary obsession. *Acorn Bluff Farms, Columbus Junction*

County fairs — Every summer, every county in a state with many celebrates bounty and craft: livestock shows, pie contests, demo derbies, rodeos. *Lee County Fair, July*

Politics — Caucuses grab the spotlight, but it's really all about county supervisor, legislature, town council. *iowastartingline.com*

LITERARY IOWA

Points of entry into the state's exceptional world of words.

THE IOWA REVIEW
Blue-chip literary magazine since 1970. Super-smart staff.

TALK OF IOWA
Charity Nebbe's bimonthly book club, via radio and podcast.

CARNEGIE-STOUT LIBRARY
Dubuque's beaux arts beauty, a temple to people's learning.

CITY OF LITERATURE
UNESCO gives Iowa City global cred, spurring many events.

DSM BOOK FESTIVAL
Sharp headliner bookings distinguish Des Moines' fest.

NORTH AMERICAN REVIEW
Nation's oldest literary journal [1815!], based in Cedar Falls.

PORCHLIGHT
Iowa City writers' retreat and hub for literary orgs.

AMES WRITERS COLLECTIVE
Classes, readings, writing groups and community support.

RESCUE PRESS
A fierce, fun small press with a big appetite for experiment.

PRAIRIE LIGHTS
The Iowa City bookstore. You know Barack shopped here.

CULTURAL INSTITUTIONS

CODFISH HOLLOW BARNSTORMERS

5013 288th Ave, Maquoketa

A 1954 whale-belly barn: unique and beloved tour stop for national musicians. In the barn, dance. On the lawn, laze by fire pits.

LOWELL AND AGNES WALTER HOUSE

2611 Quasqueton Diagonal Blvd, Independence

Also known simply as Cedar Rock, one of the most complete extant examples of architect Frank Lloyd Wright's Usonian design aesthetic.

CLARINDA CARNEGIE ART MUSEUM

300 N 16th St, Clarinda

In a state loaded with great arts institutions: a find. An old small-town library carves an elegant niche with perfectly scaled capsule exhibits.

SCENIC DRIVES AND PUBLIC LANDS

Back roads and natural sites throughout the Hawkeye State.

U.S. ROUTE 1

North, pass through Grant Wood landscapes to Solon and Mt. Vernon for antiquing and nestled culinary gems. South, head toward Kalona: antiques, farm stands, and Mennonite shops. *From Iowa City*

NEAL SMITH NATIONAL WILDLIFE REFUGE

A mesmerizing voyage into preagricultural Iowa, by way of a magic carpet of grassland to the domain of the mighty bison. *Near Prairie City*

LOESS HILLS NATIONAL SCENIC BYWAY

Threaded along Iowa's western border, a slow-drive dream links wildlands, archaeological sites, vintage towns and scenic overlooks. The Mondamin loop hike leads to wildflowers. *South from Plymouth County*

HIGH TRESTLE TRAIL

A two-wheel "drive," see. In a bike-loving state, this may be the definitive route: 25 miles through iconic Iowa countryside, centered on a half-mile-long ex-railroad trestle remade as a sprightly architectural landmark. Detour to the Cumming Tap: stop for those who know. *Woodward*

THE BRIDGES OF MADISON COUNTY

Is it even really optional? A few twists of vintage gravel farm roads and a small-town cruise link the scenes made famous by Robert James Waller's novel [not to mention Clint and Meryl, emoting in the rain]. Get a post-drive pint at The Drift. *Winterset*

BACKBONE STATE PARK

Dense and vivid intersection of nature and history. The Devil's Backbone anchors networks of hiking and cross-country ski trails, while Richmond Springs feeds some of Iowa's best trout fishing. The Civilian Conservation Corps Museum tells of bygone public spirit. *Dundee*

WESTERN SKIES SCENIC BYWAY

A doctoral-level class in Iowa landscape via 142 straight-line miles, through farms, towns, prairie and history. *From Stuart*

CULTURE

FILM

The Music Man
What's Eating Gilbert Grape?
Field of Dreams
Country
The Straight Story
King Corn
The Bridges of Madison County
Saving Brinton
Bonnie and Clyde
Cold Turkey
Storm Lake
Children of the Corn

MUSIC

Greg Brown
The Iowa Waltz

Dar Williams
"Iowa"

Julee Cruise
Floating into the Night

William Elliott Whitmore
"South Lee County Brew"

Slipknot
Iowa

BOOKS

☞ *Gilead* by Marilynne Robinson: A dying pastor weaves a tale stretching across one man's life and beyond to consider God, war, the Underground Railroad and life in a small Iowa town. A true modern American classic.

☞ *We Heard It When We Were Young* by Chuy Renteria: A big, soulful blast of Mexican American life in West Liberty and Muscatine. Basketball, censoring your Snoop rhymes when you walk past church, Lowrider Ray.

☞ *A Thousand Acres* by Jane Smiley: *King Lear* gets an Iowa makeover. Intergenerational dilemma transplants to a flat world of grain silos and country roads. The angst builds through deceptively simple, clear prose.

☞ *The Iowa Baseball Confederacy* by W.P. Kinsella: A deeper cut from the author of *Shoeless Joe* [a.k.a. *Field of Dreams*]. A baseball fan somehow slides back in time to an alternate-dimension game that goes to ... extra innings.

☞ *A Region Not Home: Reflections from Exile* by James Alan McPherson: Ruminative and rangy essays by a beloved Writers' Workshop teacher.

☞ *The Recovering* by Leslie Jamison: A young writer's memoir takes on the mythos and dark side of Iowa's literary culture.

ISSUES

Labor — In Iowa, the place that grows and processes bumper crops of food for the world, the workers behind the scenes often struggle. From an infamous immigration raid on a meat plant in Postville in 2008 to Covid deaths at a Tyson facility in Waterloo that led to court battles, worker safety and basic human rights issues collide here. Workers and advocates campaign for wage increases and legal awareness. **EXPERT:** *Maria Cachua, board member, Center for Worker Justice of Eastern Iowa*

Weather — Floods in 2008 reshaped Iowa City and other towns. In 2020, a derecho wind storm wreaked havoc on farms. Recent years have seen intense rainfall [fed by climate change] and stronger tornados. Recovery specialists urge infrastructure upgrades. **EXPERT:** *Gabriele Villarini, professor, University of Iowa College of Engineering*

Pipelines — Iowa could sit at the center of three spawling proposed carbon-capture pipelines. Doubts unite farmers and environmental advocates. **EXPERT:** *Emma Schmit, senior organizer, Food & Water Watch*

Politics — Once a prized bellweather of national normalcy, Iowa has followed larger trends of polarization between town and country. One result: the state's place at the front of the presidential nominating calendar is in doubt. **EXPERT:** *Steffen Schmidt, professor emeritus, Iowa State University Department of Political Science*

STATISTICS

622 million .... Bushels of soybeans harvested statewide, 2021
8 .... U.S. poets laureate graduated from Iowa Writers' Workshop
14,905 .... Average home attendance, U of I wrestling, 2021-22 season
28 .... Height [ft.] of Albert the Bull statue in Audubon
70 .... Types of "food on a stick" [est.], Iowa State Fair
0.1 .... Remaining percentage, virgin Iowa prairie

SELECTED CONTENT

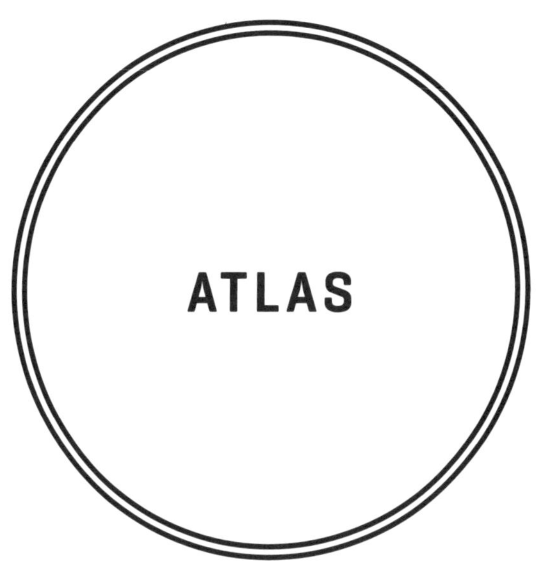

ATLAS

A guide to the lands and places of Iowa, including curated favorites, communities large and small, and a road trip from the great river's banks to the capital city

BESTS

FOOD & DRINK

ASIAN-INSPIRED

Harbinger

2724 Ingersoll Ave
Des Moines

Chef Joe Tripp and team sleuth it out in Thailand and Vietnam to stir a bright remix. Trust us: order the carrots.

NEAPOLITAN PIZZA

Lincoln Winebar

125 First St W
Mount Vernon

Wood-fired pies from a custom oven, with hyperlocal spirit. Primo beer and wine.

MIDDLE EASTERN

Oasis

206 N Linn St
Iowa City

Expat Israelis decided Iowa City needed falafel, launched a hummus kingdom.

FARMSTEAD

Cobble Hill

219 2nd St SE
Cedar Rapids

France and Brooklyn meet in IA. Check the chalkboard for the growers' roster. Super-seasonal fare, best cocktails around.

DUTCH DUEL

Jaarsma *vs.* Vander Ploeg

Pella

At stake: bragging rights on the "Dutch letter," an S-shaped butter pastry filled with almond paste.

NEW AMERICAN

Brazen

955 Washington St
Dubuque

Bouloud-trained Kevin Scharpf came home to blow minds.

HIGH COMFORT

Rodina

1507 C St SW
Cedar Rapids

The spiritual backbeat of Czech Village: hearty and beautiful cooking, family-style conviviality. Real cozy little spot.

BREADS

The Local Crumb

thelocalcrumb.com
Mount Vernon

Life-affirming, real-deal bagels and loaves from a sourdough master. Seek, find.

FANCY NIGHT OUT

The Webster

202 N Linn St
Iowa City

Smart collage of Asian, Italian and Iowa. Biscuits, fried rice, gnocchi.

MEXICAN

La Regia Taqueria
436 Hwy 1
Iowa City
Iowa's taqueria trail leads here: lengua, hot sauce mixtape, tons of cilantro and lime.

CANDY PARLOR

Wilton Candy Kitchen
310 Cedar St
Wilton
Homemade candy, phosphates and ice cream. Since 1867.

FARMSTAND

Dogpatch Urban Garden
5085 Meredith Dr
Des Moines
Summer sweet spot of fresh salads, field dinners.

SCHNITZEL SANDWICH

Ronneburg
4408 220th Trail
Amana
An Amana Colonies mainstay.

VEGAN

Trumpet Blossom
310 E Prentiss St
Iowa City
Righteous bowls, sannies, live music.

SUPPER CLUB

Timmerman's
7777 Timmerman Dr, East Dubuque, IL
Big meat, big martinis. Expansive, ultra-old-school joint on a Mississippi bluff.

VEGETARIAN

Blazing Star
120 E Water St
Decorah
Power-packed bowls full of Iowa farm goodness.

ALGERIAN

Schera's
107 S Main St
Elkader
Za'atar and bourek where you least expect 'em.

AYURVEDIC INDIAN

Gupta's
51 S Court St
Fairfield
Big veggie plates, near Maharishi Vedic Observatory.

SHAKSHUKA

Eatery A
2932 Ingersoll Ave
Des Moines
When the temps drop [as they do], this will do the trick.

COCKTAILS

The Bartender's Handshake
3615 Ingersoll Ave
Des Moines
A dreamy wood-paneled den. Up first, the curry negroni.

CIDER

Wilson's Orchard
4823 Dingleberry Rd NE, Iowa City
Crisp delights from an age-old orchard.

BIERHALL

Hessen Haus
101 4th St
Des Moines
Truly splendid import lineup.

BREWERIES

Kalona Brewing Co.
Kalona
Sucha Much IPA.

Pulpit Rock
Decorah
Pizza Roulette.

Lion Bridge
Cedar Rapids
Bohemian Premium.

Big Grove
Solon, etc.
Easy Eddy IPA.

LODGING

CITY STAY

Surety Hotel

Des Moines

suretyhotel.com

Classic design swagger in a 1913 building. Perfect lobby for posting up, writing the next *Gatsby*.

THROWBACK

Hotel Julien

Dubuque

hoteljuliendubuque.com

Grande dame with beaux arts beauty, Capone lore.

CULTURE HUB

Hotel Chauncey

Iowa City

hilton.com

Indie cinema FilmScene is *in* the building. Walk to art museum, readings.

INDUSTRIAL CHIC

Hotel Millwright

Amana Colonies

hotelmillwright.com

Mod aesthetic at a working textile mill.

ARCHITECTURE ICON

Historic Park Inn

Mason City

historicparkinn.com

Last surviving hotel designed by Frank Lloyd Wright. Prairie Style on the prairie: right angles for days.

HISTORIC CRED

Hotel Blackhawk

Davenport

hotelblackhawk.com

A mainstay dating to 1915, lately reborn after many a zigzag. Cary Grant's last stop.

MAIN STREET USA

Hotel Winneshiek

Decorah

hotelwinn.com

Downtown heartbeat, with 1905 roots and on-site opera house.

RETRO COOL

Highlander Hotel

Iowa City

highlanderhotel.us

Snazzy reboot of a '70s hang, centered on a swank pool.

LOCAL LANDMARK

The Warrior Hotel

Sioux City

thewarriorhotel.com

An art deco survivor in a city noted for the style, reborn in 2020. Rooftop bar, lavish decor, bowling alley!

SMALL-TOWN BOUTIQUE

Hotel Grinnell

Grinnell

hotelgrinnell.com

Former junior high gets a striking, art-forward makeover.

FARMSTAY

Little House on the Farm

Postville

littlehouseonthefarm.com

Salvaged barn, cozy cabin, kitties and cows.

EXCURSION STOP

Hotel Pattee

Perry

hotelpattee.com

Zany themed rooms, perfect for Raccoon River Trail cyclists.

OUTDOORS

TRUE PRAIRIE
Rolling Thunder Prairie
South of Des Moines
A Warren County preserve of rich habitat and native grasses, 200 acres never plowed.

PADDLING
Upper Iowa River
Put in at Bluffton
Storied in the region, rich in wildlife, limestone bluffs and cool old bridges.

FISHING SHOP
Rod & Rivet
Des Moines
rodandrivet.com
The state's go-to fly outfitter is the source for gear, trout intel.

BIRDWATCHING
Cone Marsh
Conesville
iowabirds.org
Ducks, geese, shorebirds, wading birds, the occasional water pipit, all the snipe.

BIG BIKE RIDE
RAGBRAI
ragbrai.com
Iowa loves cycling, in large part because of this 50-year-old festival on wheels, crossing the state every summer.

NOT-AS-BIG BIKE RIDE
Farm Cycle
Iowa City
icbikelibrary.org
Mixed ability levels, stops where chefs serve food from farms, on farms.

BIKE SHOP
Goldfinch
Cedar Rapids
goldfinchcyclery.com
Worker-owned spot with a full range of steeds, services.

GRAVEL RIDE
Octagonal Barn Loop
Iowa City
bikeiowa.com
Country ramble past a historic barn.

SKATEBOARDING
Lauridsen Skatepark
Des Moines
dsmskatepark.com
One of the largest in the nation, home to a Dew Tour pro event and rails, ledges, pools galore.

NORDIC SKIING
Trout Run Trail
Decorah
visitdecorah.com
Eleven miles of groomed trails, with good options for all skill levels.

DAYHIKE
Ledges State Park
Madrid
A 4-mile trail delves into dramatic, canyon-like terrain and CCC history.

WEEKEND BACKPACK
Yellow River State Forest
Harpers Ferry
Driftless Area woods and streams; well-marked 25-mile trail.

SHOPS

MENSWEAR

Fontenelle Supply

524 E Grand Ave
Des Moines

Burly yourself up with artisan U.S.A. brands chosen with expert eye, and leather goods crafted in-house.

GIFTS

AKAR Design

257 Iowa Ave
Iowa City

Big, airy shop with that bright, Scandi-style gleam. High-design *objets* for home, office and self.

KITCHENWARE

Cooks' Emporium

313 Main St
Ames

When Le Creuset calls, this fave dating to 1979 answers.

FARM & HARDWARE

Fisk Farm & Home

Monona, Cresco and Decorah

Poultry, horse and herd essentials.

SEEDS

Seed Savers

3074 N Winn Rd
Decorah

Heirloom veggie aces. Here you'll find Joe's Big Blocky Red, Principe Borghese, Di Sicilia Violetto, Table Queen, Nadapeno.

WOMENSWEAR

Marnē

350 E Locust St
Des Moines

Perhaps the chicest dresses and sweaters on the prairie, plus vegan sneakers and boots.

FURNITURE

Mad Modern

227 16th Ave SE
Cedar Rapids

Sharp midcentury staples and killer art.

PLANTS

Pots & Shots

9500 University Ave
Des Moines

Plants and cocktails: anthurium meets amaro. Not mad.

GENERAL STORE

Des Moines Mercantile

3707 Sixth Ave
Des Moines

Premium-grade everything, from quilts to candles to the nicest lint brush you'll find.

VINYL

Record Collector

116 S Linn St
Iowa City

An old-school crate-diggers' gem. Trust the taste level here.

MIDWEST PRIDE

Raygun

Des Moines, Davenport, etc.

Iconic source for whipsmart swag.

BOOKSTORES

Book Vault
Oskaloosa

River Lights
Dubuque

Next Page
Cedar Rapids

Swamp Fox
Marion

ARTS & CULTURE

ARTS FESTIVAL

Mission Creek

Iowa City

missioncreekfestival.com

Perhaps unique: a springtime collision of indie music and literary arts, powered by A-list talent.

DESTINATION

American Gothic House Center

Eldon, americangothichouse.org

Homestead background for Grant Wood's painting. Deep interpretation.

SCULPTOR

Annick Ibsen

annickibsen.com

Vivacious clay work with strong cubist influence.

ART CLASSES

Gilchrist Center

Sioux City

siouxcityartcenter.org

Four studios in a luminous building.

CRAFT SHOW

Norwegian-American Folk Art Exhibition

Decorah

vesterheim.org

Fine handmade goods and art pieces, notably knives and rosemaling.

FILM FESTIVAL

DSM Latino Film Festival

Des Moines

latinocenterofiowa.org

Multiday showcase of international and local creators.

PUBLIC ART

Thomas F. Agran

Iowa City

thomasagran.com

Bold, big murals, technical panache.

PODCAST

Iowa Basement Tapes

Tireless show from Des Moines' KFMG, documenting indie and underground Hawkeye State music.

MUSIC SERIES

Feed Me Weird Things

Iowa City

feedmeweird.com

Strange, challenging, heart-quickening live music of all descriptions [and none].

MUSEUM

Dubuque Museum of Art

dbqart.org

The state's oldest art institution is strong on Midwest creators and ambitious new work by Iowans.

THEATRE

Riverside Theatre

Iowa City

riversidetheatre.org

Adventurous shows, plus free summer Shakespeare.

CONDUCTOR

Joseph Giunta

dmsymphony.org

Up front for Des Moines' fine symphony, 34-plus years.

EVENTS

ICE CREAM

Ice Cream Days

Le Mars

icecreamdays.com

Le Mars stakes a claim as "Ice Cream Capital of the World." [Blue Bunny's based here.] Seems suspicious, better fully investigate.

WRESTLING TOURNEY

Soldier Salute

Coralville

soldiersaluteia.com

Grappling showdown for men and women debuted in 2022.

CORN

West Point Sweet Corn Festival

West Point

@wpcornfest

On a magic Sunday in August, free sweet corn, 11 a.m. till ??.

BASEBALL

Iowa Cubs

milb.com

International League action brings in spring.

POWWOW

Meskwaki Annual Powwow

Tama, meskwaki powwow.com

More than a century old, the August festival of Iowa's only recognized tribe showcases dances, songs, regalia.

FARMING HERITAGE

All-State Barn Tour

iowabarn foundation.org

Statewide effort to save endangered barns shows 'em off.

BUFFALO

Bison Fest

Council Bluffs

pottconservation.com

Botna Bend Park's small but feisty herd is the focal point of science, craft activity.

ANTIQUES, ETC.

What Cheer Flea Market

What Cheer

One of the Midwest's best. Can't beat name.

CURED MEATS

Blue Ribbon Bacon Festival

Des Moines

blueribbon baconfestival.com

Many themes, but always a return to home truths: bacon and beer. Questions?

TUG-OF-WAR

Tugfest

Le Claire vs. Port Byron

tugfest.com

Two towns. Two teams. One river [the Mississippi]. One rope [2,700 feet].

KITES

Color the Wind

Clear Lake

Huge, extravagant flying creations above the February snow.

PUPPETS

Great Plains Puppet Train

West Liberty

Shows, how-to workshops.

EXPERTS

PRAIRIE REVIVAL

Justin Meissen
Tallgrass Prairie Center
Bringing native plants and habitats back, one roadside strip and farmland patch at a time.

PORK

Kathy and Herb Eckhouse
laquerciashop.com
Founders of America's premier proscuitto brand, champions of Iowa heritage hogs.

INDIGENOUS LANGUAGE

Wayne Pushetonequa
meskwaki.org
Revitalizing and teaching Meskwaki via events, classes and mobile apps.

AMISH HISTORY

Nancy Roth
kalonaiowa.org
Historic village and insights on faith communities, pioneer life.

COMMENTARY

Lyz Lenz
lyz.substack.com
Pugnacious, pungent words on culture and politics from a reporter/memorist with deep Iowa cred.

BOOKMAKING

Julie Leonard
juliealeonard.com
Director of UI's Center for the Book learned her craft in a mountain cabin, creates strange beauty.

GRAPHIC NOVELS

Lauren Haldeman
@laurenhaldeman
Poet/artist with a winsome eye for soccer-playing animals and haunting story.

HOSPITALITY

Angela Harrington
highlanderhotel.us
The state's only female hotelier leads smart renovations of historic properties in towns big [for Iowa] and small.

FARMING

Grimm Family Farm
North English
Three generations, no pesticides. Chickens, dried beans, and produce from English River fields.

Practical Farmers of Iowa
practicalfarmers.org
Training, resources and support for small family farmers in the land of Big Ag.

POLITICAL REPORTING

Clay Masters
iowapublicradio.org
Public radio staple, co-creator of the 2019 podcast *Caucus Land*, host of the homegrown *Morning Edition*.

LOCAL PUBLICATION

Little Village
littlevillagemag.com
Zesty news, biz, food coverage for Cedar Rapids, Iowa City.

CITIES & TOWNS

From cities rich in lore to small towns stocked with unexpected finds, Iowa's communities are famed for hospitality and creativity.

IOWA CITY

Iowa City rises out of farmland like a bohemian vision; in the words of Andre Perry, writer and arts orchestrator: "A good place to get stuff done." The indie cinema **FILMSCENE** stands as one beacon, bringing in the new and curating classics. The **STANLEY MUSEUM OF ART**, opened in 2022, puts down a serious marker with Jackson Pollock's *Mural* and keeps going with vivid contemporary arts, photography and print collections. On campus, the **ANA MENDIETA GALLERY** in the stunning Visual Arts Building showcases student work; nearby, Arts Building West's cantilevered library is secretly the coolest place in town to sit and read. A long walk in **HICKORY HILL PARK** helps settle the day before cocktails and top-tier Americana fare at **PULLMAN DINER**.

BIG SHOWS	
Englert Theatre	POPULATION: 74,596
Touring talent, galas and a classic marquee	COFFEE: Tru
	BEST DAY OF THE YEAR: Witching Hour arts fest, autumn

DECORAH

Decorah represents the heart of the Driftless Area, a landscape that escaped the glaciers that turned most of the Midwest into crop-friendly flatlands. Here, rolling hills and valleys remain full of cold-water trout streams and crunchy-creative humans. You'll encounter all at **SEED SAVERS**, a sprawling farm with public trails and fishing spots alongside a seed bank specializing in rare heirlooms. Norwegian roots and liberal arts anchor Decorah, thanks to **LUTHER COLLEGE** and mainstay bookstore **DRAGONFLY**. Renowned brewery **TOPPLING GOLIATH** is known for flagship Pseudo Sue pale ale and Kentucky Brunch Brand Stout, instantly selling out at $100 per bottle. [The beer is just as good at the newer Pulpit Rock, founded by two TG alums.]

FOLK ART	
Vesterheim	POPULATION: 7,747
Deep study of traditional Norwegian craft	COFFEE: Impact
	BEST DAY OF THE YEAR: Decorah Time Trials biking, April

DES MOINES

Iowa's capital marks the crossroads of interstates 80 and 35, plus the confluence of two vital rivers. The East Village nurtures artisan boutiques like **KIN** and refined eats and drinks: head to **PURVEYOR**, home of cured meats and fine wines, and Alba for gussied-up Americana. Like any capital city, DSM has its monuments, among them the wonderworld of **GREATER DES MOINES BOTANICAL GARDEN**. But **EL BAIT SHOP** and its staggering array of more than 250 beers might be our favorite attraction. Festivals take over downtown much of the year, including the 80/35 Music Festival each July and the **WORLD FOOD & MUSIC FESTIVAL**, a September bow to harvest and global culture, in a farm city with big dreams. That's Des Moines.

MOUNTAIN BIKING

Central Iowa Trail Assn.
Keepers of many miles of urban single-track

POPULATION: 212,031

COFFEE: Horizon Line, Daisy Chain

BEST DAY OF THE YEAR: The epic farmers' market, May to Oct.

MASON CITY & CLEAR LAKE

You may know Mason City by its stage name, River City. Meredith Wilson based 1957 Broadway smash *The Music Man* on his hometown; his boyhood home on Music Man Square gives tours. More pilgrims, however, come here for the **PARK INN HOTEL**, Frank Lloyd Wright's last remaining hotel; Rock Crest-Rock Glen National Historic District claims the country's tightest grouping of Wright-inspired **PRAIRIE SCHOOL** buildings. The architect's students designed most of them, after the man himself skipped town with a client's wife. To cool off from that hot gossip, Clear Lake lies 10 miles west, suffused with beachy vibes. The storied **SURF BALLROOM** hosted the final show of Buddy Holly, Ritchie Valens and The Big Bopper in 1959, and still books bands. Commune with the spirits in this undersung arts crossroads.

STEAKHOUSE

Northwestern Steakhouse
By Iowa consensus, the state's family-run best

POPULATION: 27,138

COFFEE: Three on the Tree

BEST DAY OF THE YEAR: Iowa Independent Film Festival, September

DUBUQUE

Along the horizon, steeples and smokestacks merge with ridgelines, with a view into Wisconsin and Illinois. For the easiest summit, hop inside the Alps-inspired cable car, **FENELON PLACE ELEVATOR CO.** [An 1880s mayor built this "world's steepest, shortest scenic railroad," allegedly to nap at home over lunch.] In town, the thing to see: the Tiffany stained glass at St. Luke's United Methodist, a triumph of sacred vision. Kevin Scharpf's **BRAZEN** [farm-to-table with Italian accents] anchors the Millwork District. Rooms at **HOTEL JULIEN** promise a historic overnight. A hotel since 1839, it's named after French-Canadian trader Julien Dubuque, who arrived in 1785 to found one of the oldest European settlements west of the Mississippi.

BEER	POPULATION: 59,119
Dimensional Brewing	COFFEE: Jitterz
Industrial-chic digs, many IPAs and sours	BEST DAY OF THE YEAR: DBQFest arts and music, August

SIOUX CITY

Iowa's far-west outpost once also answered to "Little Chicago" for its booming meatpacking business, stately architecture and noted wild side. The place still has gravitas. **WOODBURY COUNTY COURTHOUSE** stands as one of the greatest Prairie style buildings, adorned with streamline moderne work by Chicago sculptor Alfonso Iannelli. The Loess Hills, a natural treasure snaking down the SoDak/Nebraska border, intersect with Sioux City at **STONE STATE PARK**, woods and grasslands full of Civilian Conservation Corps buildings. Virginia Square is home to restaurant **TABLE 32**; for an older-school experience, seek out the signature Twin Bings of **PALMER CANDY**. The newly restored Warrior Hotel, an art deco and terra-cotta wonder, anchors the fusion of history and possibility.

OLDTIME FINDS	POPULATION: 85,617
Antiques on Historic Fourth	COFFEE: Hardline
Many vendors gather at the heart of a 19th-century neighborhood	BEST DAY OF THE YEAR: River-Cade Parade, July

CEDAR RAPIDS

Iowa's second city has a cozy, homey feeling. [Dare it be said, especially when the air smells of Crunch Berry? Much of America's breakfast cereal is made here.] In the 1850s, Czech folk fleeing European turbulence found refuge, and the **CZECH VILLAGE AND NEW BOHEMIA** district remains a pocket of beautiful painted doorways and murals, kolache bakeries [**SYKORA**] and entrepreneurial vigor. Take it in at Cafe Saint Pio, a coffee shop of throwback charm and fine cappuccino. **NEWBO CITY MARKET** gathers a score of artisans and food purveyors. Dobry stocks discerning home goods, and **NEXT PAGE** picks the right new books. Absorb the backstory on this Euro-American crosshatch at the **NATIONAL CZECH AND SLOVAK MUSEUM & LIBRARY**, notably strong on decorative arts and photography from the Old Country.

LIVE SHOWS	
Ideal Theater	POPULATION: 136,467
A knockout restoration of a 1914 cinema, with luxe bar	COFFEE: Dash
	BEST DAY OF THE YEAR: NewBo Art Fest, Labor Day

AMES

Iowa State University's base is an intellectual powerhouse. The **AMES NATIONAL LABORATORY**, a Nobel-winning hub with roots in the Manhattan Project, keeps on inventing new materials and fuels. Somewhere else on the campus-life spectrum, the **MAINTENANCE SHOP** holds down a spot on the college-rock circuit dating the '70s. **PROVISIONS LOT F** wraps together a sprawling all-day menu, omelettes to pizza to cocktails; **THE CAFE** is a bedrock farm-to-table spot with 20 years of local buy-in. And while State's research makes it an engine of Big Ag, more downhome visions still thrive: **BLACK'S HERITAGE FARM** offers a vintage field wander, veggie share or pumpkin patch outing.

ART CLASSES	
Octagon Center for the Arts	POPULATION: 66,424
Throw on the wheel, illustrate on screen	COFFEE: Morning Bell
	BEST DAY OF THE YEAR: State Science and Technology Fair, March

GRINNELL

Grinnell feels like a town where you could craft your own story in so many different ways. Threads of the plot converge at **SAINTS REST COFFEE**, where the ear catches oldtimer talk of the soybean harvest and the eye catches the rack of indie magazines and art show flyers. A college town, maybe? Indeed. **GRINNELL COLLEGE**, a liberal arts school of alt-Ivy League caliber, dates to the 1840s. Campus life to keep you talking all year: the ambitious theater and dance department shows, and the Division III basketball program, famed for its frenetic "**GRINNELL SYSTEM**" playing style. [In one game in 2022, the Pioneers attempted 111 three-point shots. True story.] Get the Iowa Chop at the **PRAIRIE CANARY**, do your vintage shopping at **POWESHIEK TRADING POST**: you're halfway to being a citizen here.

SCIENCE & NATURE	
Center for Prairie Studies *Grinnell's program focused on tallgrass ecosystems and cultural history*	POPULATION: 9,513 DONUTS: Grin City Bakery BEST DAY OF THE YEAR: Grinnell Games sports fest, June

QUAD CITIES

Davenport. Bettendorf. Rock Island, Moline and East Moline in Illinois. Two states, five cities, but... "Quad Cities"? Go with it: A key Mississippi River nexus birthed this bistate metro. [Throwback sports buffs, recall the NFL's Rock Island Independents and the NBA's Tri-City Blackhawks. Johnny Cash fans, shout out "Rock Island Line."] A longtime music hotbed is going strong at Davenport's **RACCOON MOTEL** and **REDSTONE ROOM** and Rock Island's bold **ROZZ-TOX**. The **FIGGE ART MUSEUM** boasts deep Grant Wood archives. Quad Cities-style pizza is its own deal,: malt in the crust, pepper flakes in the sauce. Local chain **HARRIS PIZZA** stakes its claim. Before, during or after any outing, a stop at **MAC'S TAVERN** [est. 1934] is likely in order.

MUSIC EDUCATION	
Common Chord *Mentorship, camps, live shows and music-scene advocacy*	POPULATION: 379,172 [metro] COFFEE: Milltown BEST DAY OF THE YEAR: Bix Beiderbecke Jazz Festival, August

ROAD TRIP

Journey through hills and prairie, starting at a great river, looping through small cities with big cultural voices.

DAY 1

PIKES PEAK AND THE EFFIGY MOUNDS

In ways both literal and cosmic-metaphorical, Iowa begins where the Mississippi carves through lands deep with history and natural beauty.

8 A.M. The edge-of-Iowa perch of limestone ridge and sheer dolomite known as **PIKES PEAK** is named for the same Zebulon Pike of the more famous Colorado mountain. Look down on the Mighty Mississippi's earth-moving force from 500 feet up, with the Upper Mississippi River Valley stretching beyond.

9 A.M. Hiking trails thread through Pikes' leafy slopes; the go-to reaches **BRIDAL VEIL**, a rare Iowa waterfall. Others traverse caves and explore mounds built by Indigenous people more than 1,000 years ago.

11 A.M. Pikes' ancient structures are just a warm-up for **EFFIGY MOUNDS NATIONAL MONUMENT**, a short jaunt north, and its 200 or so mounds, built over centuries by Indigenous people. [Today, 20 Native tribes are affiliated with the monument.] Some of the grassy structures outline profiles of bears or birdlike creatures, the largest known collection of such effigies in the U.S. To delve into the story, snag a tour with a ranger for the 2-mile hike along Fire Point Trail. Or just head straight for **GREAT BEAR MOUND**, 137 feet long and 70 feet wide.

2 P.M. The riverside roads hold their own attractions, especially idyllic river towns McGregor and Marquette. In McGregor, antiquarian-leaning **RIVERTOWN FINE BOOKS** and gift shop **PAPER MOON** hold down Main Street storefronts, an easy stroll from lunch at **THE OLD MAN RIVER RESTAURANT & BREWERY**.

4 P.M. **MARQUETTE**'s Eagles Landing Winery works with cool-climate grapes suited to Iowa: Seyval blanc, or the Iowa-developed Petite Pearl. Anglers, detour 2 miles west—or book a night of camping—along gorgeous **BLOODY RUN CREEK**. The spring-fed river teems with trout, perfect for wade-fishing.

MANSION: Villa Louis **TOUR:** Maiden Voyage **INN:** Little Switzerland

THE FIELD OF DREAMS

The ghost of Shoeless Joe Jackson may [or may not] emerge from the corn, but the romance of a classic, bucolic baseball scene is alive and well.

"If you build it, he will come." Kevin Costner's character, Ray, hears that whisper through the corn in *Field of Dreams*, a trophy of late-'80s cinema built on a novel by W.P. Kinsella. [ICYMI: Farmer builds baseball diamond in cornfield, summons ghosts of 1919 Chicago White Sox.] Folklore made the quote plural, and the movie indeed turned a Dyersville farm into a pilgrimage site. Nostalgic seekers can stroll the *Field* diamond, get in a game of catch, even rent the farmhouse for a stay. In 2021, the big leagues arrived for real in the form of the modern-day White Sox and New York Yankees. After a 2022 reprise, the state announced plans to fund a permanent stadium at the site—a happy meeting of promotional mojo and sincere Americana worthy of the movie's key question: *Is this heaven? No, it's Iowa.*

At MAQUOKETA CAVES STATE PARK, *follow lighted pathways through* 1,110*-foot-long Dance Hall Cave, then traverse towering Natural Bridge. Brave visitors bring headlamps for smaller nooks.*

DAY 3

IOWA CITY'S WRITING WORLD

No disrespect to New York, Boston or any other readerly spot, but this college town just might be America's capital of bookishness.

Worldwide, writers ask, "Why is everyone talking about Iowa City?" At a glance, the University of Iowa's base looks like a handsome Big 10 football town on the prairie. But literature weaves through the city's genes. Flannery O'Connor honed her chops here. Kurt Vonnegut and Saul Bellow partied. Young talent like Jamil Jan Kochai and Sarah Thankam Mathews makes Iowa City a present-day farm team for the National Book Awards.

The singular reason: the IOWA WRITERS' WORKSHOP, famed fiction and poetry graduate program. The Workshop HQ at DEY HOUSE is not an all-hours attraction but frequently hosts visiting authors for events in its Reading Room. In a bigger way, the Workshop anchors a university steeped in the creation and culture of the word. Notably, the INTERNATIONAL WRITING PROGRAM keeps a steady beat of readings, talks and film screenings, just part of a packed citywide literary calendar. Another source for the datebook: THE CENTER FOR THE BOOK, the university's department studying "the book arts," i.e., papermaking, bookbinding, letterpress. Gallery shows and talks focus on the book as both object and craft.

Any reader's Iowa City ramble will start at PRAIRIE LIGHTS, nationally beloved bookstore, right downtown. Amid three floors, the poetry section stands out; the cafe serves as writerly Iowa City's second office. Minutes' walk away, find a different vibe at THE HAUNTED BOOKSHOP, an atmospheric 10-room jumble of used books in a house dating to 1847. Across town, Sidekick Coffee & Books tilts toward kids and young readers.

LITERARY TAVERNS

GEORGE'S BUFFET
A place of forever twilight, all-season Christmas lights and famed cheeseburgers. Some sources call this the "poets' bar."

DAVE'S FOX HEAD TAVERN
In this telling, the Fox Head is the fiction-writers' bar. But paths cross: Seamus Heaney and Jeffrey Eugenides once duelled at pool.

DAY 4

THE IOWA STATE FAIR

Over two weeks every August, a sprawling celebration of Iowa draws more than one million fair-fans. Longtime CEO Gary Slater helps navigate the midway.

ACTION

Slater ranks the array of **LIVESTOCK SHOWS** high on the list. "If you win Champion Bull here, it's as prominent as winning the Western Stock Show in Denver," he says. Pioneer Livestock Pavilion dates to 1902.

FOOD

"Your food journey": that's how Slater describes the odyssey of fried Twinkies, Cattlemen's Beef Quarters burgers, and everything on a stick. [**PORK CHOP ON A STICK** is a presidential campaign perennial.] Hot tip: "The **CORN DOG** is king."

ICON

The fair's butter sculpture tradition—low-moisture Iowa sweet cream, please—goes back more than a century. Only five artists have created the signature **BUTTER COW**. Current sculptor Sarah Pratt apprenticed for 15 years. "It's like your mother sent you to church," Slater says of this singular thing you've gotta see.

DAY 5

THE DES MOINES DAY

Land in the state's very heart with a day out in Iowa's version of the big city: coffee, art, shopping and food.

MORNING Start at **HORIZON LINE**, a shining West End coffee spot, where the milk comes from Iowa cows and mocktails mingle tea or espresso with seltzer and fruit. Just a block away, **PAPPAJOHN SCULPTURE PARK** anchors this end of downtown with nationally significant work by Ugo Rondinone, Louise Bourgeois and many others. [Jaume Plensa's *Nomade*, a gorgeous, looming human form fashioned from latticed stainless steel, is the go-to snapshot.] Two miles west on Grand Avenue, the affiliated **DES MOINES ART CENTER** traces a global contemporary aesthetic—free admission for Hopper, Bacon and much else. Gray's Lake Park, just south of downtown, boasts a beach and picturesque 2-mile loop trail.

AFTERNOON The East Village, clustered around the State Capitol, marks Des Moines' crossroads of creativity. Daisy Chain Coffee provides the second-wind burst of energy that may come in handy, nestled next to local icon **RAYGUN**, pretty much a legend for its witty, politically pointed T-shirts and ephemera that proclaim Midwest pride in all-caps sans serif. Up the way, **FONTENELLE SUPPLY CO.** crafts rugged leather goods in its open workshop in back, stocking well-chosen artisan menswear brands up front. **STORYHOUSE BOOKPUB**, possibly the cutest micro-den for sharply curated new books, puts on popular double-feature author events. For something more physically vigorous, **ADVENTURE ROCK** climbing gym accepts walk-ins, all gear included with admission. [Conveniently, it shares a parking lot with Peace Tree Brewing.] Franka provides the artful pizza.

EVENING The first thing a proud Des Moinesian will say: The food scene is seriously on the rise. **HARBINGER** usually gets next mention for chef Joe Tripp's veggie-focused Asian interpretations—pho-inspired cocktails, steamed buns in glorious variety. As the night goes on, **THE LIFT** is the hole-in-the-wall you might not expect: martinis, art, adventurous live music. [Nearby, all-time great neon marks Fong's Pizza. See for yourself.] **HELLO, MARJORIE**'s classic cocktails and Iowa beers put a blue ribbon on the day.

GRAIN BOWL: St. Kilda | **GALLERY:** Moberg | **DIVE BAR:** Locust Tap

SELECTED CONTENT

MORE THAN 30 ENTRIES ☞

Excerpts have been edited for clarity and concision.

A deep dive into the cultural heritage of Iowa through news clippings, timelines, writings and other historical hearsay

CORN

A prairie country has a fascination which to the careful observer equals or excels that offered by a mountainous district. There is, to be sure, nothing arresting, nothing magnificent and compelling such as we find in mountain visits or vast encircling barriers of hills, but rather a subtle charm which increases as one becomes more familiar with it. The prairies are never perfectly level, there are almost imperceptible gradations in the surface which lead the eye on and on to where some farmstead with its grove marks the horizon. There are Corot-like lines of single trees marching across the landscape, for your prairie farmer is as devoted to straight lines as any Cubist. The fields, under the pale spring sun, seem already full of promise of a rich harvest. ...

Early tho' the season is, one thought possesses the farmer to the exclusion of all others—the corn. At intervals during the winter he has looked with anxious eyes at certain strings of plump yellow ears of corn, hanging in a safe dry place: the machine-shed, an old house or perhaps even in one of the bedrooms. There have been farmers who held their seed corn so dear that they have actually hung it in their own bedrooms and have slept the winter through in a bower of gold, reminiscent of past harvest and eloquent of abundance to come.

Very early, in April, perhaps even in March, the careful husbandman begins his testing, urged thereto by the newspapers which through columns of figures trumpet the direful results attendant upon planting untested corn. The ways of testing are manifold, there are certain attractive machines for the purpose upon the market, but the ordinary farmer uses a box of earth or sawdust dampened and covered with a cloth marked into squares, each of which is numbered. Five or six kernels of corn, carefully selected from the butt, the tip and the center of the ear are placed on a square and the ear is numbered to correspond. In a few days the dampened kernels sprout and one is able to ascertain if the germination is good, fair or poor.

When the results are known, the sheep are separated from the goats, the good ears are carefully saved and the poor ones are thrown out to be used as feed. —*Hortense Butler Heywood* [1884-1977], *noted entomologist and historian, born in Cherokee, Iowa. This account is preserved in the archives of Iowa State University.*

FRANK GOTCH

Chicago Tribune, April 5, 1904

"GOTCH WINS WORLD'S WRESTLING CHAMPIONSHIP BY MAKING 'RUSSIAN LION' QUIT"

Frank Gotch, the greatest wrestler America ever has produced, last night relegated George Hackenschmidt, the "Russian Lion," to the ranks by forcing him to quit at the end of what was probably the most desperate mat battle in the history of wrestling. The struggle of Titans began at 10:29 o'clock, and exactly two hours and one minute later Hackenschmidt, the conqueror of the Terrible Turks, held helpless on the mat, raised one hand in token of defeat. Gotch released him immediately. Hack approached Referee Ed Smith and said, "I surrender the championship of the world to Mr. Gotch." The referee at once named Gotch as the new king. The plucky Iowan only smiled and accepted Hackenschmidt's proffered hand. The crowd of 6,000 spectators became frenzied with delight.

Born on a Humboldt farm, trained by "Farmer" Martin Burns of Cedar County, Frank Gotch became one of his era's most famous athletes. The National Wrestling Hall of Fame's Dan Gable Museum in Waterloo commemorates Gotch and other Iowa grappling legends.

KURT VONNEGUT

Assignment letter to Writers' Workshop students, 1965

Beloved: This course began as Form and Theory of Fiction, became Form of Fiction, then Form and Texture of Fiction, then Surface Criticism, or How to Talk out of the Corner of Your Mouth Like a Real Tough Pro. It will probably be Animal Husbandry 108 by the time Black February rolls around. As was said to me years ago by a dear, dear friend, "Keep your hat on. We may end up miles from here." As for your term papers, I should like them to be both cynical and religious. I want you to adore the Universe, to be easily delighted, but to be prompt as well with impatience with those artists who offend your own deep notions of what the Universe is or should be.

THE IOWA WRITERS' WORKSHOP

1922 .... U of Iowa: nation's first to award creative advanced degrees
1936 .... Media theorist Wilbur Schramm starts Workshop
1941 .... Paul Engle, Cedar Rapids poet, takes over the graduate-level program for fiction and poetry writers
1940s ..... Workshop sessions meet in unheated Army quonset huts
1945 .... Engle mansplains sex scenes to Flannery O'Connor
1947 .... Robert Penn Warren: first faculty member to win Pulitzer
1950s ..... Donnelly's Pub: hangout for John Irving, Dylan Thomas
1955 .... Poet John Berryman fired for drunken incident [look it up]
1959 .... *Esquire* Iowa City writing panel: Mailer and Ellison headline
1960 .... Engle gets $40K Rockefeller grant. Some later theorize sinister corporate/government sway over Iowa writing.
1963 .... Raymond Carver enrolls but doesn't thrive
1965 .... Kurt Vonnegut teaches, writes *Slaughterhouse Five,* throws famed parties on North Van Buren
1967 .... Vonnegut on Engle: "hayseed clown," "foxy grandpa," other words not for print
1970 .... *Iowa Review* publishes first issue
.... MFA for David Milch, creator of *NYPD Blue, Deadwood*
1973 .... Carver, John Cheever are now Iowa writing profs. Carver: "He and I did nothing but drink."
1974 .... Fresh off Berkeley homeless stint, future legend Denis Johnson gets MFA
'76-'77 .... MFA bumper crop: Jane Smiley, Rita Dove, T.C. Boyle
1978 .... Novelist Sandra Cisneros graduates; later calls Workshop "rather horrible"
.... Joy Harjo, future poet laureate, graduates
1987 .... Frank Conroy becomes director, serves until death in 2005
.... Ann Patchett and Lucy Grealy are student roommates
1995 .... Novelist/doctor Ethan Canin, an alum, joins faculty
1997 .... Workshop moves into present home, Dey House
2006 .... Lan Samantha Chang [*Inheritance,* etc.] becomes director
2008 .... UNESCO proclaims Iowa City a "City of Literature"
2011 .... 75th anniversary keynote delivered by Marilynne Robinson, Pulitzer winner, professor emerita
2022 .... Workshop alum Brandon Taylor wins Story Prize

HERITAGE FESTIVALS

MAIFEST

Carrying on the German tradition of celebrating spring, Maifest brings out Maipole dancers, a parade, German music and food. *Amana Colonies, May*

TULIP TIME

A town renowned [and themed] for Dutch heritage celebrates with street scrubbing, tulip gardens, Dutch foods and more. Dates back to 1935. *Pella, May*

HOUBY DAYS

Czech yourself: live music, food vendors, games, and—of course—a kolache-eating contest. Houby [HOE-bee] translates to "mushroom" in Czech. *Cedar Rapids, May*

I'LL MAKE ME A WORLD IN IOWA

Live music, Black history presentations, dinner and dancing. Michelle Williams, Shemar Moore and Kenny Lattimore have all headlined. *Des Moines, winter*

JULEFEST

Everything a Danish Christmas could be: homemade treats, Christmas markets, hot drinks. *Elk Horn & Kimballton, November*

TIVOLI FEST

Held over Memorial Day weekend, the annual Danish celebration includes folk dances and, of course, a Viking encampment. The Museum of Danish America takes the story much deeper. *Elk Horn, May*

NORDIC FEST

Since 1967, Decorah has marked its Scandinavian history with Nordic Fest. The Vesterheim, the nation's Norwegian American museum, lines up the music, craft, swordplay. *Decorah, July*

GERMANFEST CELEBRATION

Biergarten, homemade beer tasting, a kraut cookoff, wiener dog races. *Guttenberg, September*

PRAIRIE WILDFLOWERS

PURPLE PRAIRIE CLOVER *Dalea purpurea* A thimble-shaped purple flower on a wiry stem; most widespread perennial prairie clover.

GRAY-HEADED CONEFLOWER *Ratibida pinnata* Recognizable by droopy yellow flowers around a gray to brown central disc. Blooms early July and August.

BLACK-EYED SUSAN *Rudbeckia hirta* Bright-yellow, daisy-like flowers can grow to be 2 feet tall. Iowa City's official flower.

WILD BERGAMOT *Monarda fistulosa* Pink or purple pom-pom flower. In the mint family, so also known as "bee balm" or "horsemint," if you prefer.

BUTTERFLY MILKWEED *Asclepias tuberosa* Iowa's most colorful milkweed. Also known as "pleurisy root," due to Indigenous use: chewed to treat pulmonary ailments.

CUP PLANT *Silphium perfoliatum* Stout leaves create a small cup around the stem that holds water, attracting birds.

ROSINWEED *Silphium integrifolium* Tall, drought-resistant, sunflower-like plants. Bloom all summer and into the fall.

COMPASS PLANT *Silphium laciniatum* So named because they orient north or south to avoid the noonday sun. Can grow up to 6 feet tall.

PRAIRIE BLAZING STAR *Liatris pycnostachya* A spike of dense, purple stalkless flower heads. *Pycnostachya* is Greek for "crowded."

RATTLESNAKE MASTER *Eryngium yuccifolium* Unusual spiny, yucca-like leaves make this plant unpalatable to livestock. Once thought to have a variety of curative powers.

LONGBRACT SPIDERWORT *Tradescantia bracteata* Blue or purple petals, once thought to cure spider bites. Blooms June to August.

PARTRIDGE PEA *Chamaecrista fasciculata* Delicate leaves collapse when touched. Extrafloral nectaries produce nectar outside of the flower.

JESUS' SON

Published in 1992, this short-story volume by Writers' Workshop alum Denis Johnson influenced a generation of writers with fringe characters, elegiac tone and rough locales—including The Vine, based on an Iowa City tavern. Reflections on work, setting and author, who died in 2017:

"I was living in Iowa City at the time, and this book, for my friends and me, became sort of a young writers' bible. ... The plots go like this: A man shaves his roommate in the hospital, the shave-ee having survived being shot three times by two different wives; there's one about a hospital orderly mopping a floor that's already clean, and another with a guy out on bail drinking at The Vine [a bar I could see from my apartment window ...]. And, even better, when you read them, the stories might sound like this: 'I went out to the farmhouse where Dundun lived to get some pharmaceutical opium ...' Or like this: 'We lay down on a stretch of dusty plywood in the back of the truck with the daylight knocking against our eyelids and the fragrance of alfalfa thickening on our tongues.'" —NATHAN ENGLANDER, "Writer Finds a Fated Friend in *Jesus' Son*," NPR

"The original Vine served its last whiskey a few decades ago. In the late '60s, when it was the first bar the police checked in search of perpetrators of drug-related crimes, the patrons proudly called themselves 'freaks.' It was among those freaks that Johnson found both comrades and future characters for his stories. The Mill, where he made a deal with the bartender for his 'sixty-dollar Chevrolet, the finest and best thing I ever bought,' is only a memory as well. The Mill is also where Johnson sat at the bar and, as the cigarette smoke swirled, making the air nearly unbreathable, matched drinks and talked about writing with Raymond Carver late into the night." —TED GELTNER, "When the Streets Had No Plaques: Denis Johnson in Iowa City," *Los Angeles Review of Books*

"In Iowa City, where I had friends [Iowans, I should clarify, not anyone from the Writers' Workshop], bar talk was all about Denis Johnson and *Jesus' Son*. 'He told and retold those stories until his delivery was perfect, and at that point, he wrote them down,' a crackhead I knew said to me. I later asked Denis Johnson if this was true of his process: No, it was not true. 'I just wrote them the normal way,' he said, 'one sentence at a time.'" —RACHEL KUSHNER, "Earth Angel," *The Hard Crowd*

BIX BEIDERBECKE

Quad City Times, April 25, 1928

"Bix Beiderbecke, perhaps the finest trumpeter in the country, will now play for you his own composition, 'In a Mist.'" This simple announcement in the Paul Whiteman orchestra broadcast in the midnight program over the national networks from New York Tuesday night electrified the Davenport listeners-in, and most of all a little family group in the B.H. Beiderbecke home, 1934 Grand Avenue. Their son, Leon, was that same "finest trumpeter." But six months ago he joined Paul Whiteman's orchestra after repeated requests from that famous jazz leader. His reticence was due to the fact that he played by ear and scarcely knew one note from another. Now he is a soloist and a composer, this latter with the aid of a fellow musician who wrote the score as he played it. "Bix" as he was known by the gang, and there was always a gang of 'fellers' with him in his boyhood days, has displayed his jazz tendencies since his earliest youth. He was known as a jazz artist in every school he attended but beyond that school had little appeal and he had no inclination to go on to college. Music lessons, too, were too much like a grind. He took piano lessons for a time from two local instructors, not more than a score in all. He had wonderful promise, his teachers said, but he veered away from the labor of learning. What was the sense of droning "one, two, three, four" when you could rattle off the latest jazz tune thru a magic sense entirely apart from mathematics?

Leon "Bix" Beiderbecke [1903-1931] *honed his musical chops, in part, by sitting in with bands on steamboats calling at Davenport. The Bix Beiderbecke Jazz Society pays tribute to the "hot jazz" genius with an annual summer festival in Davenport.*

COUNTY FAIRS OF NOTE

MIGHTY HOWARD COUNTY FAIR .... Cresco, *June*

GREAT JONES COUNTY FAIR .... Monticello, *July*

CLAY COUNTY FAIR .... Shelton, *September*

MISSISSIPPI VALLEY FAIR .... Davenport, *August*

WINNESHEIK COUNTY FAIR .... Decorah, *July*

TRIFLES

A Play in One Act by Susan Glaspell
Presented by the Provincetown Players at the Wharf Theatre,
Provincetown, Massachusetts, August 8, 1916

SCENE: *The kitchen in the now abandoned farmhouse of John Wright, a gloomy kitchen, plainly left without having been put in order—unwashed pots under the sink, a loaf of bread outside the bread-box, a dish towel on the table—other signs of incompleted work.*

COUNTY ATTORNEY: Tell now just what happened when you got to the house.

HALE: I didn't see or hear anything; I knocked at the door, and still it was all quiet inside. I knew they must be up, it was past eight o'clock. So I knocked again, and I thought I heard someone say "Come in." I wasn't sure, I'm not sure yet, but I opened the door, this door [*jerking a hand backward*] and there in that rocker—[*pointing to it*] sat Mrs. Wright. [*All look at the rocker*]

COUNTY ATTORNEY: What—was she doing?

HALE: She was rockin' back and forth. She had her apron in her hand and was kind of—pleating it.

COUNTY ATTORNEY: And how did she—look?

HALE: Well, as if she didn't know what she was going to do next. And kind of done up.

COUNTY ATTORNEY: How did she seem to feel about your coming?

HALE: Why, I don't think she minded—one way or other. She didn't pay much attention. I said, "How do, Mrs. Wright, it's cold, ain't it?" And she said, "Is it?"—and kind of went on pleating at her apron. Well, I was surprised; she didn't ask me to come up to the stove, or to set down, but just sat there, not even looking at me, so I said, "I want to see John." And then she—laughed. I guess you would call it a laugh. I thought of Harry and the team outside, so I said a little sharp: "Can't I see John?" "No," she says, kind o' dull like. "Ain't he home?" says I. "Yes," says she, "he's home." "Then why can't I see him?" I asked her, out of patience. " 'Cause he's dead," says she.

Susan Glaspell, born in Davenport and educated at Drake, co-founded the Provincetown Players and is credited with discovering Eugene O'Neill. She based Trifles *on a murder trial she covered as a Des Moines newspaper reporter. Long neglected, it is now regarded as a feminist classic.*

KUM & GO

Milestones of Iowa's roadside staple.

1959 UI journalism school grad William Krause gets smart, goes into the gasoline business with father-in-law T.S. Gentle

1963 Partners introduce "station store" idea: Hampton spot now sells gas *and* other merchandise

1975 "Kum & Go" unites *K*rause & *G*entle's expanding empire of locations under one brand name

1977 The company counts 65 locations, more than 300 employees

1988 HQ moves from Hampton to West Des Moines

1990s Buyouts of struggling 7-Elevens and Git'N Gos fuel further expansion across Iowa

2006 Johnny Knoxville sports Kum & Go shirt in *Jackass Number Two*. Merch sales boom.

2009 Company Twitter account @kumandgo begins reaching the "kummunity." Yes, it's funny.

2015 "Not Overlooking the Kum & Go" by Iowa Writers' Workshop-trained poet D.A. Powell: *All underage kids must come here. And go here? / The world rhymes with itself.*

2018 Company headquarters, Krause Gateway Center, opens in Des Moines; design by acclaimed architect Renzo Piano

2020 Kum & Go parent company buys Italian professional soccer team Parma Calcio 1913

Tanner Krause, age 33, takes over as fourth-generation CEO

Urban, walk-up, no-gas "godega" concept opens in Des Moines

2021 Kum & Go's TikTok account attracts following thanks to very witty 20-year-old creator Evelyn Meyer

2022 Ownership group awarded minor-league soccer franchise for the Des Moines Menace, home of the Red Army

Expansion plans include Idaho, Michigan, Utah locations and 900-plus hires

BREAKFAST AND SNACKS

In Cedar Rapids, two titans turn Iowa farm bounty into iconic products.

GENERAL MILLS

Lucky Charms [1964]
Auspicious marshmallows, sugared oats.

Honey Nut Cheerios [1979]
Rare sequel to surpass original.

Fruit by the Foot [1992]
B. Crocker-branded roll-ups.

Betty Crocker Frosting [1963]
Breakfast can mean many things.

QUAKER OATS

Quaker Oats [1877]
Arguably, the national porridge.

Quaker Grits [1967]
U.S. Patent no. 3,526,512.

Cap'n Crunch [1963]
Archenemy: Jean LaFoote.

Life [1961]
Real ones roll Original, like Mikey.

Cedar Rapids citizens speak of "Crunch Berry days," when the Cap'n Crunch spin-off leaves the air "fruity and delicious." Lion Bridge Brewing's Crushberry Sour pays homage.

HOT AIR BALLOONS

Entrants, 2022 National Balloon Classic, Indianola.

FLAMETASIA
AIR FORGE
CZECH-MIX
VAGABOND
PIXIE STIX
KAY'S WINDDANCER II
PINK PANTHER
GOLDEN GRIFFIN III

2PINK4U
SEW GRATEFUL
RED DAWN
MIDNIGHT MASQUERADE
ZENITH STAR
TWISTED TRUTH
DREAM DUSTER
FORGET ME KNOT

FLAME BUOYANT
XTREMELY CONTAGIOUS
ORANGE CRUSH
SUNSATIONAL
JOYOUS PLEASURES
N DA DOGHOUSE
NIGHT BREEZE
CHAMPAGNE SUPERNOVA

BETTER HOMES AND GARDENS

Vol. 1, Issue 1, July 1922
"A Little Garden in the City"
By Lilian Hall Crowley

A GARDEN! That was the thing Miss Josephine Wallace wanted most of all when she looked out on the barren yard behind her home on a busy city corner in Des Moines. A garden was the very thing, but she had scarcely a place in which to make one. She looked at the yard and was a bit discouraged at the sight, and her family laughed outright at the idea that anything could be made of the place. Then she thought that even a greater joy of making a garden might come from having practically nothing to begin with and in making a garden in a ramshackle, old backyard.

She planted for constant bloom. For the early spring there were borders for the bulb beds, borders of blue scillas and yellow crocuses and snowdrops. She planned and planted beds of rose-pink, enchantress-pink, wedgewood-blue, and yellow hyacinths, narcissi in shades of yellow, and red and rose-colored tulips. In this planting are early and late tulips. In this little garden were seven thousand bulbs. These earlier flowers were followed by iris, peonies and phlox.

While Miss Wallace was making her garden she realized more than ever the joy of friendship, for friends who would not have had time to make a call, in passing would peek thru the lattice and stop for a moment's conversation. Many would go thru the artistic little gate and chat for awhile asking questions while Miss Wallace continued her work and explained her plan.

It isn't given to everyone to be an artist. At the same time, realize that a garden is something which should be enjoyed by everyone. The reason I wanted to tell you about this little garden is that it just shows better than anything else what can be done in spite of unfavorable conditions. While space may be small, even smaller than this, beauty is by no means limited to a large and wide expanse of plantings.

Founded by Edwin Meredith—former Secretary of Agriculture, proprietor of newspaper Farmer's Tribune *and son of Avoca, IA—* Better Homes and Gardens *has democratized American design for* 100 *years. [Meredith called the magazine "the common meeting place."] Lilian Hall Crowley was active in Iowa's suffrage movement.*

ANA MENDIETA

The artist Ana Mendieta [1948-1985] immigrated to Iowa as a child, a refugee from Cuba. Immersed in the innovative University of Iowa arts programs of the 1970s, she created work now recognized as an intersection of land art, multimedia and feminist expression. After moving to New York City, she was killed in a fall from the Greenwich Village apartment she shared with her husband, Carl Andre. [Andre was acquitted of murder charges, but the incident remains a source of heated contention in the art world and beyond.] Commemorating a creative career launched in Iowa City, the university dedicated its Ana Mendieta Gallery in 2022.

SELECT IOWA PERIOD WORKS & WHERE TO SEE THEM

BLOOD SIGN #1
Super-8 film, 1974
Animal blood: a major motif
Art Institute of Chicago

IMAGEN DE YAGUL
Photograph, 1973
Body obscured by greenery
SFMOMA, San Francisco

UNTITLED [MOFFITT BUILDING]
Super-8 film, 1973
Passersby see mysterious blood
Walker Museum, Minneapolis

The 2022 podcast Death of an Artist *examined Mendieta's legacy.*

THE DAY THE MUSIC DIED

The Globe-Gazette, Mason City, February 4, 1959

The three nationally famed rock 'n' roll singers who died with their pilot, Roger Peterson of Clear Lake, in a Tuesday morning crash had quite a following among Mason City teenagers. That was evident after a check with the city's phonograph record dealers. Although news of their tragic deaths was only hours old, discs recorded by Buddy Holly, Ritchie Valens and J.P. Richardson [The Big Bopper] were already in extra-heavy demand Tuesday afternoon. A Mason City radio station popular with the teen set, too, was giving special attention to Holly, Valens and Big Bopper tunes.

Buddy Holly was 22 at the time of the crash; Ritchie Valens was 17 and The Big Bopper was 28. Other musicians on the same tour took the bus to Fargo, and played the next night.

GROTTO OF THE REDEMPTION

"On March 15, 1928, in the little town of West Bend, Ia., a minister of the gospel began one of the greatest construction jobs of its kind ever attempted in the Christian world. Today, after a little over 14 years, the work still continues. Already it has entailed a journey of over 100,000 miles to every state in the United States as well as some foreign countries to gather material to be used in its construction. Already, although it is only half completed, it has attracted over two million visitors from all parts of the world. When completed 'The Grotto of the Redemption' will rank with Taj Mahal in India as one of the seven wonders of the modern world. Taj Mahal was built for the love of a woman. The 'Grotto' is being built for the love of Christ. In building the Grotto of the Redemption, the Rev. Mr. Doberstein hopes to further the word of God by producing in stone a considerable portion of the Bible. Sixty-four carloads of stones, petrifications, corals, etc., have been gathered for this purpose from the 48 states of the nation and from many foreign countries. These are being set in concrete in carefully arranged patterns to portray the Garden of Eden, Stable of Bethlehem, Calvary Mount, the Tomb, the Resurrection and hundreds of other biblical scenes. This is one place that must be seen to be appreciated. The greatest story of all time is told eloquently in stone."
—*Bethany Republican-Clipper*, August 26, 1942

THE IOWA CAUCUSES

1968..... Chaotic protests at Democratic Convention in Chicago spur changes to presidential primary system

1971..... Iowa Democratic operative Richard Bender redesigns traditional precinct nomination meetings

1972..... Iowa debuts as first-in-the-nation state; Maine's Ed Muskie wins Dem caucus, George McGovern gets surprise second place

1976..... GOP joins Iowa process. Jimmy Carter becomes first "outsider" to win in Iowa on the way to the White House

1980.... George H.W. Bush takes surprise win over Ronald Reagan; falls short of nomination, but Iowa gets Bush on the VP road

1984.... On Democratic side, strong Gary Hart showing rattles frontrunner Walter Mondale, preview of Reagan landslide

1988..... Bob Dole and Pat Robertson push Republican frontrunner Bush into third. Democratic field: a Trivial Pursuit question.

1992..... Iowa senator Tom Harkin dominates; future president William Jefferson Clinton gets just 2.8 percent

1996..... Eventual GOP nominee Bob Dole runs nearly neck-and-neck with populist Pat Robertson

2000.... Big wins for George W. Bush and Al Gore set the stage for a ... somewhat complicated year

2004.... "Dean Scream" in a West Des Moines ballroom: random mic moment seen as downfall of Howard Dean's outsider campaign

2008.... Barack Obama stuns Hillary Clinton. To Iowa supporters: "You have done what the cynics said we couldn't do."

2012..... Republicans Rick Santorum and Mitt Romney nearly tie in vote total, but Ron Paul works the intricate Iowa tabulation process to win most delegates in the end

2016..... After second-place finish, Donald Trump tweets: "Ted Cruz didn't win Iowa, he stole it." Hillary beats Bernie Sanders by 0.2 percent.

2020.... Mobile app snafu delays Democratic results by three days, muting Pete Buttigieg win over Sanders. Joe Biden in fourth.

2022..... Democrats move to change nominating calendar to de-emphasize Iowa; Republicans stick with first-in-nation status

BONNIE & CLYDE

Des Moines Tribune, July 24, 1933

3 OF BARROW GANG ESCAPE POSSE; REPORTED FLEEING IN KOSSUTH COUNTY

A three-hour intensive search near Panora for three suspected members of the notorious Barrow brothers gang was ended at 1 p.m. Monday by a posse of more than 50 men. The hunt had centered near Panora when it was reported that a car with a woman who had a bandaged head was seen driving that way. Later it was found that no one actually had seen the bandit car near Panora.

CAPTURED. Earlier in the day, a man and woman identified as Mr. and Mrs. Marvin Barrow were captured in a wooded tract near Dexter, after they had been left behind by companions, two men and a woman. The sheriff of Kossuth county later Monday reported to the state bureau of investigation that the Barrow gang had been seen passing through Luverne, Ia.

HEADED EAST. The car, headed east, was driven by a woman. Three men also were in the car, the sheriff reported, one of whom was lying down, apparently wounded. The car was said to be the Chevrolet coach stolen earlier Monday at Polk City. The license is 77-13662. The three who escaped are believe to be Mr. and Mrs. Clyde Barrow and Jack Sherman, members of the desperadoes wanted for Missouri murders and holdups.

RILEY WOUNDED. C.C. [Rags] Riley of Des Moines, Polk county deputy sheriff, was wounded slightly in the head early Monday morning in an exchange of shots between all five members of the bandit gang and a posse north of Dexter. After the three members of the bandit gang had escaped from near Dexter, they commandeered a car from a farmer and sped to Polk City. There they held up an oil station and took the attendant's car. The abandoned machine was bloodstained and the windshield was shattered.

The Texas outlaws Bonnie Parker and Clyde Chestnut "Champion" Barrow gained national infamy as the center of a murderous stickup gang in the Depression-era heartland. After escaping the Iowa dragnet, they headed south, dying in an ambush in Louisiana, in May 1934.

AMERICAN GOTHIC

In 1930, painter Grant Wood, raised in Anamosa and Cedar Rapids, made a painting of a man, a woman and a country house with a surprisingly fancy window. Today, American Gothic *draws visitors to the 1880s house in Eldon, first sketched by Wood after an outing with a fellow artist. As models, the painter drafted his sister and his dentist, sketched in separate sessions, far from the house itself. Some read* Gothic *as a satiric dig at rural life; others, as a somber evocation of Depression-era struggle. Whatever the interpretation, it may be the nation's most recognizable artwork. Three reflections:*

STEVEN BIEL

American Gothic: *A Life of America's Most Famous Painting* 2005

Wood painted *American Gothic* in three months. He started with a thirty- by twenty-five-inch piece of relatively cheap beaver board, made from compressed wood pulp and used in construction for walls and partitions. He applied a white foundation, now yellowed where it wasn't covered with other paint [especially in the boards of the house], and drew an outline of the picture in black. Then he filled it in, laying thicker textures on the house and overalls, lighter textures in more delicate strokes on the faces.

NAN WOOD GRAHAM

My Brother, Grant Wood 1993

Grant assured us both that ... no one would ever recognize us. He told me to slick down my hair and part it in the middle, and asked me to make an apron trimmed with rickrack, a trim that was out of style and unavailable in the stores. After the painting made its debut, rickrack made a comeback.

GRANT WOOD

Letter to Nellie Sudduth 1941

The persons in the painting, as I imagined them, are small town folks, rather than farmers. Papa runs the local bank or perhaps the lumber yard. He is prominent in the church and possibly preaches occasionally. In the evening, he comes home from work, takes off his collar, slips on his overalls and an old coat, and goes out to the barn to hay the cow. The prim lady with him is his grown-up daughter. Needless to say, she is very self-righteous like her father. I let the lock of hair escape to show that she was, after all, human.

The painting hangs in The Art Institute of Chicago, which provides excellent online interpretation: artic.edu.

WORLD FOOD PRIZE

Select honorees

1987 M.S. Swaminathan [India] .... *High-yield wheat, rice*
1989 Verghese Kurien [India] .... *Boosting India milk production*
1991 Nevin Scrimshaw [U.S.] .... *Development of nutrition-rich foods*
1993 He Kang [China] .... *Ag minister: self-sufficiency reforms*
1994 Muhammad Yunus [Bangladesh] .... *Microloans, expanding food access*
1999 Walter Plowright [U.K.] .... *Rinderpest vaccine*
2002 Pedro Sanchez [U.S.] .... *Improving Global South soil fertility*
2008 Bob Dole, George McGovern [U.S.] .... *Global school foods campaign*
2017 Akinwumi Adesina [Nigeria] .... *African agriculture reform*
2021 Shakuntala Thilsted [Trinidad] .... *Fish-farming improvements*
2022 Cynthia Rosenzweig [U.S.] .... *Climate-change impact studies*

Awarded annually in Des Moines, the WFP is akin to a Nobel for nutrition and agricultural studies. It honors Norman Borlaug, pioneering agronomist, born and raised in Cresco, IA.

STORM LAKE TIMES-PILOT

Founded in 1990 *with the Cullen family as its core, the* Storm Lake Times-Pilot *serves as a tireless watchdog in the land of Big Ag. The paper's* 2017 *exposé on corporate-funded water litigation won the Pulitzer Prize.*

From "Attracting Young People," Editorial, 2022

If you could build a more diverse food system that valued people and communities, perhaps people would value rural life. Iowa is not really putting its shoulder into it, because our state leadership is beholden to interests whose main concern is exploiting rural resources and people who have no leverage. You gain leverage through education. ... If we had the greatest pre-K-12 schools in the world, if college debt weren't a barrier, if we embraced immigrants, if we reoriented agriculture toward healthy food and communities, and if you could build a bike trail around Storm Lake and revive the community concert series, you no doubt will have a better shot at revitalizing rural Iowa. Until then, the familiar exodus of talent that would prefer to stay closer to home will continue.

OCTAVE THANET

From The Man of the Hour [1905]

In the early eighties Fairport considered herself a city; but she was, in fact, an overgrown, delightful town sprawling among the low hills of the Mississippi Valley. Near enough the town's origin still to distinguish its outlines, but remote enough to idealize them, the old settlers were a power, and could be found of a sunny afternoon at Luke Darrell's livery stable, busy with the apotheosis of the days when they shot quail before breakfast; true brotherly love prevailed between men; and the river was the highway of commerce. Despite the pioneers' lamentations, Fairport was a kindly town, where every one went to the High School before his lot in life gave him college or work for his daily bread; and old acquaintance was not forgot. Like most middle-western towns, it was touched by all the great issues of the world. This, indeed, is the significant trait of western life; to feel vividly things which concern not the petty affairs of the individual, but the welfare of the commonwealth or the race.

"Octave Thanet" was the pen name of Davenport-reared Alice French [1850-1934], an eminent novelist and short-story writer of her time. French and her life partner, Jane Allen Crawford, divided their time between Arkansas and Davenport, where today the public library's archives contain a collection of their papers.

HOBO KINGS

The National Hobo Convention in Britt crowns subcultural monarchs. Honor roll:

HAIRBREADTH HARRY
SCOOP SHOVEL SCOTTY
HIWAY JOHNNY WEAVER
CANNONBALL EDDY
PENNSYLVANIA KID
BEEF STEAK CHARLIE
STEAMTRAIN MAURY
SLOW MOTION SHORTY
FRY PAN JACK
RAMBLIN' RUDY
FISHBONES
EL PASO KID
SONGBIRD MCCUE
SIDEDOOR PULLMAN KID
LIBERTY JUSTICE
NEW YORK SLIM
BO GRUMP
REDBIRD EXPRESS

HOMER DILL

"EXPEDITION MAKES HIGHLY INTERESTING REPORT"

The Daily Iowan, September 26, 1911

Having been gone for a period approximating two months, the Laysan Island expedition, sent out under the auspices of the university of Iowa the past spring, arrived in Iowa City during the latter part of the summer, with a wealth of scientific material and a host of experiences and memories. ... All in all it was unquestionably one of the greatest achievements of modern science and an undertaking, which, to date, has been advertised far and wide, and bids fair to attract the attention of the scientific world for years to come. Aside from the collections of birds and animal life made on the island, which comprised a total of thirty-six large cases weighing almost a ton, the members brought back with them an impression which is to be molded into a great scenic vista, or cyclorama, an exhibition of colossal proportions. ... Birds almost without number were collected and skinned, Professor Homer R. Dill facetiously explaining that "we skinned birds from morning till night."

Homer R. Dill was a pioneering taxidermist and naturalist, collaborator of the noted University of Iowa zoologist Charles Cleveland Nutting. The Laysan Island Cyclorama still exists, one of the last displays of its kind, in the university's natural history museum. A sharp essay on Dill by Inara Verzemnieks can be found in the anthology Best American Nonrequired Reading 2016.

JESSE JAMES

Des Moines Register, July 30, 1873

From a detective who had been in pursuit of the robbers of Chicago, Rock Island & Pacific road: Two of the gang are the James boys, of Clay county, Missouri, the same party which robbed the Chariton and Clarendon banks. ... The James brothers crossed the Hannibal and St. Joseph railroad at Kidder last Friday before daylight on their way south, evidently going to their mother's house. ... This Jesse James is known to be the chief of a gang of robbers which is a terror from Clay county to Sherman, Texas. Indeed, when it is known they have committed any depredations, everyone gives up further effort to capture them.

IOWA FOODWAYS

TENDERLOIN Pork, that is. Pounded thin, bigger than an LP record, breaded, fried, served on a bun about one-third its size.

BREAKFAST PIZZA White sauce, scrambled eggs, breakfast meat. Casey's Gas Station speciality.

FROG EYES Ham or corned beef, rolled around cream cheese and pickle spear, sliced crosswise.

TACO PIZZA Happy Joe's Pizza's pride. Crushed tacos [shell and all] on pizza, drizzled with taco sauce.

SCOTCHEROOS Chocolate-topped butterscotch Rice Krispies treat. All grandmas make the best.

MAID-RITE Loose meat sandwich from the original Muscatine location, est. 1926.

PALMER TWIN BING Sioux City candy legend. Creamy, cherry-flavored nougat patty coated in chocolate and peanuts.

WALKING TACOS Open bag of Fritos or Doritos. Fill with seasoned ground meat, taco toppings. Crush. Eat out of bag.

SNICKERS SALAD Cool Whip, Snickers, caramel drizzle, Granny Smith apples.

STERZING'S POTATO CHIPS Made in Burlington. Extra greasy. Fresh daily since 1930s.

CAFETERIA CHILI In some schools, chili comes with a cinnamon roll. In others, a peanut butter sandwich.

EURO-IOWAN DELICACIES

Lefse: *A Norwegian potato crepe.*
Kolache: *Czech pastry. Like a Danish, but … not Danish.*
Dutch letters: *Buttery, flaky cinnamon pastries, sometimes shaped like family initials and sometimes shaped like an* S, *for* Sinterklaas [*Santa Claus*].

INCLUDED

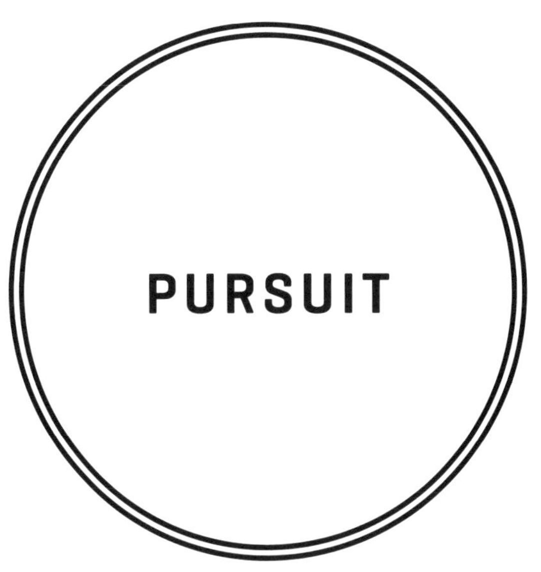

PURSUIT

A field guide to writing and the teaching of writing in Iowa, with craft tips on fiction and poetry, insight on Iowa City's unique literary heritage and key inspirations

FOUNDATIONS

It is a fair question: How did Iowa, land of corn and county fairs, become a noted hotbed for writers? The story stretches from the state's origins to the most recent bestseller lists.

HISTORY

Even as 1830s settlers plowed prairie into farmland, Iowa's river of printed words began to flow. The *Du Buque Visitor,* the future state's first newspaper, appeared in 1836 with a lofty vow of neutrality and rectitude [unfulfilled, they say]. Two years later, Iowa Territory's first governor talked of a library, stocked with essential books, and soon it came to be. The university in Iowa City embraced creative arts from its early days. [Iowa State, meanwhile, grew from the first of the nation's great land-grant colleges.] Farming journals, practical and feisty, quietly made Des Moines a publishing town. By 1897, University of Iowa students could enroll in "verse-making"—traditions of craft and teaching firmly rooted.

CULTURE

Today, there is the Writers' Workshop, attracting an exceptional number of writers to Iowa City. [Scottish novelist Margot Livesey: "I was buying petrol in Iowa City. The attendant asks what I do. 'I teach at this place called the Writers' Workshop.' He immediately asks, "Fiction or poetry?""] But other literary enterprises dot the state like so many prairie lights. Tireless small publishers [Ice Cube Press]. Classic little magazines [*Eastern Iowa Review,* Shellsburg]. Heartfelt booksellers [Soul Book Nook, Waterloo]. Fascinating digital experiments [*Guesthouse*]. As with every state, Iowa has a lot going on. Unlike most any other, it also has a highway rest stop emblazoned with a Vonnegut quote [Tiffin].

> *"The emergence of Iowa as a conscious intellectual and literary region gave rise some years ago to the phrase, 'the Iowa Renaissance.' It has not been a renaissance in any sense of the word: there has been nothing to be reborn from, but only a long and slow awakening, through three generations of writers."*
>
> —**WALLACE STEGNER**, "The Trail of the Hawkeye," 1938

WRITING PROGRAMS, PRIZES & PUBLICATIONS

IOWA SUMMER WRITING FESTIVAL Call it the people's Workshop: a summerlong cycle of themed writing workshops, open to all. Weekend, weeklong, two-week intensive. Fiction, poetry, memoir, more. Hundreds come to Iowa City, top-tier instructors taking the lead. *iowasummerwritingfestival.org*

IOWA STATE MFA IN CREATIVE WRITING & ENVIRONMENT Iowa City is not the state's sole literary center. Iowa State's rich research legacy informs a three-year program on writing about place, nature, science and the human role in all of the above. The program runs its own 76-acre nature preserve. *engl.iastate.edu*

SUSAN GLASPELL WRITERS & CRITICS SERIES In Des Moines, the Drake University English Department stages a diverse series of open mics, readings, workshops and roundtables. Storytelling, flash fiction, poetry, songs. *drake.edu*

KRAUSE ESSAY PRIZE The U of Iowa Nonfiction MFA Program selects one standout piece every year. Past winners—Wesley Morris, Oliver Sacks, Mary Ruefle, etc.—are an unofficial masterclass. *krauseessayprize.org*

IOWA SHORT FICTION AWARD Any writer who has not yet published a full-length work of prose fiction can throw in for Workshop-run prize. *uipress.uiowa.edu*

GRINNELL COLLEGE Iowa's beacon of small-town progressive education brings in all-star teachers, notably in its "Short Course" program [Garth Greenwell, Lan Samantha Chang]. *Grinnell Review* publishes twice annually. *grinnell.edu*

MAGID CENTER PUBLICATIONS UI's undergraduate writing center produces many publications, including *Boundless*, a journal of multilingual translations, the single-page monthly *New Moon* and speculative fiction magazine *Wilder Things*. *magidcenter.uiowa.edu*

SPANISH-LANGUAGE MFA Iowa is one of few U.S. schools offering a full creative writing MFA in Spanish. The program publishes online journal *Iowa Literaria*: original works, contemporary poetry translations. *iowaliteraria.lib.uiowa.edu*

THE WRITING UNIVERSITY The podcast's deep archive gathers craft lectures from the Summer Writing Festival.

THE IOWA WRITERS' WORKSHOP

A time-honored center of excellence, redefined.

Dey House stands out on campus, an 1857 homestead amid the University of Iowa's blocky modern buildings. Floors and stairs creak, a photocopy machine grinds, books are everywhere. The home of the Iowa Writers' Workshop, oldest and most famous creative writing graduate school, strikes a true eccentric-hideaway note. "When I applied to the program, I was told this is like the lost city of Atlantis," says Sasha Khmelnik, Workshop graduate and now assistant director. "It's just a magical thing that forms."

There's mystique, for certain. Since its 1930s origins, the Workshop has reigned as the top finishing school for authors and poets, its faculty and alumni lists studded with boldface names. In the new century, particularly under director Lan Samantha Chang, this institution has steadily remade itself. One big, oft-repeated knock on the Workshop is that it's *too* influential, imposing a sameness on writers. [One critical article: "How Iowa Flattened Literature."] Of course, there's plenty of room for debate, ideally conducted across town at the Fox Head. But recent graduates seem quite varied in outlook and style. Yaa Gyasi's *Homegoing* begins in 18th-century Ghana; Kiley Reid's *Such a Fun Age* takes place in the contemporary Philadelphia suburbs; Lee Cole's *Groundskeeping* is a well-regarded novel about Kentucky and the search for home. The present-day student body is far more international and [some say] collegial than in the past.

Unchanged: the powerful allure of Iowa to aspiring creators.

"I don't think people always appreciate what the Midwest has to offer," says Chang, a Guggenheim-winning fiction writer in her own right. "Intimate communities, sincere readers and citizens, a really fine community."

Famously difficult to get into, the Workshop consists of about 100 students, with critique and ambition at its core. "They put writing at the center of their lives for two years," Chang says. "That creates a wonderful creative spark, generative energy, friendship and community."

Jamel Brinkley, Iowa graduate and author of two acclaimed short-story collections, now teaches in the program. He describes his workshop sessions as forums for individual students' voices and close examination of craft. "The most important thing is to build a sense of comradery and trust in the group," Brinkley says. "People come here to be creative, and it's a place that completely opens its arms to that creativity."

"Everyone takes what feeds them," Chang says. *writersworkshop.uiowa.edu*

FICTION

Tips on practice and storytelling from Writers' Workshop teachers.

MARGOT LIVESEY [*The Boy in the Field, Criminals*]

ON GETTING STARTED: Have a routine: some part of your day or your week that you set aside. Try to read differently. Go back to some of the stories and novels you've loved and read them much more slowly, thinking about the decisions the author is making on each page. Don't pigeonhole yourself. Don't immediately start saying, "Oh, I'm a very slow writer," or, "I'm a very fast writer," or, "I can only write between 9:00 and 11:00." Keep your mind open to the possibilities.

ETHAN CANIN [*Emperor of the Air, A Doubter's Almanac*]

ON POINT OF VIEW: Point of view is not who is telling a story, but why a story is being told. That answers every question. Where do you end a short story? Where the character would end it. Where do you start the story? Where the character would start it. Every single word either sucks you deeper into the illusion, or kicks you out of the illusion. When you read, that is the illusion of being somebody else. And that is point of view.

ON DIALOGUE: If you can't say something nasty, don't say anything at all. Dialogue is conflict. Conflict has a very broad definition. Flirtation is usually conflict: prod and counter-prod. If there's not conflict in a sense, then it shouldn't be written as dialogue..

JAMEL BRINKLEY [*A Lucky Man, Witness*]

ON SETTING: Setting can feel like pure background. You can imagine some cardboard props on a stage. Setting is crucial. Your setting in many ways is your story. It enables your story, or limits your characters. It presses upon them, it constrains them, it sets them to scale. I'll go through a story with a really interesting setting that's maybe underutilized, and I'll look at page five, page eight, page 13 and see how the setting on page one is forgotten about.

ON CHARACTER: When you write a main character, you're automatically on the side of that character. But to make the story as rich as possible, try to be on the side of all your characters. Especially the ones who are not your main character. Maybe secondary characters are stripped of autonomy, doing things that are just functions of the plot. I'd say, "Is this what this character would really say? Is this what this character is really thinking?"

MARILYNNE ROBINSON

An instructor at the Writers' Workshop since 1991, *novelist Marilynne Robinson teaches a famed seminar on* Moby-Dick. *Here, select highlights from writer* Drew Bratcher's *experience:*

The class took place on Wednesday afternoons in the Frank Conroy Reading Room. On one side, tall windows overlooked the frozen Iowa River. On another, glass bookcases displayed titles by alumni: Flannery O'Connor, Wallace Stegner, Denis Johnson, Anthony Marra, Yiyun Li. As Robinson assumed the lectern, a staid hush enveloped the space.

She spoke in long, coruscating sentences whose turns and trajectories were polished and unpredictable. She quoted Tyndale and the day's *Times*. She read from Jonah, referenced Augustine, Dickinson, Heisenberg, Locke. She was up on cosmology, phenomenology, history and linguistics. How to describe her voice? Dulcet, untroubled. Not trying to sell you anything. She wore a clip-on microphone, the projection of which was interrupted each time her argent hair fell across her shoulder. Even after the hair was pushed back, the pitch of her voice was such that you felt yourself leaning in. Indeed this is one of my abiding impressions of the class, of a kind of gravitational pull toward the lectern.

Her paperback copy looked like an overstuffed drawer. It was bent beyond repairing. Every other page was flagged. She had read the novel countless times, she had taught it repeatedly, but she had yet to shed her astonishment. To hear her read long passages, sometimes laughing to herself, sometimes hovering over certain turns of phrase, was to be given access to a private enthusiasm. In response to a line from a chapter called "The Sphinx"—"An intense copper calm, like a universal yellow lotus, was more and more unfolding its noiseless measureless leaves upon the sea"—she sighed and said, "What can we say? He had a gift." This was how to read *Moby-Dick*: slowly, expectantly, with amusement, with gratitude.

In 2015, *Barack Obama asked Robinson about the protagonist in her novel* Gilead, *a male pastor in rural Iowa. Her response:*

"I was surprised that I was writing from a male point of view. But there he was. … He just showed up. And the first things that I knew about him—that he was old, that he had a young son, and so on—they create the narrative."

POETRY

Tracie Morris began teaching poetry at the Workshop in 2017. "It's not a question of having a good idea," she says of her teaching style. "Everybody has a good idea. It's helping that idea emerge with as much integrity and rigor as possible." Another rule of thumb: "It's not the writing; it's the editing." She shares a hypothetical example:

Let's say a student brought in a line: *Look at all the little, tiny, pretty things.*

I'd ask the student, "Why do we need *all*? If we need *all*, do we need *all the little*?"

You have *look*, *little* and *tiny*. So many *L*s and so many *T*s. It's going *L-T-L-T-T*. The sharpness of those consonants makes it sound really, really small.

And then I might ask, "Is it *that* small? How small are we talking about here? You're saying *look*, right? That implies the naked eye. Is it that small?"

Let's try: *Look at all the little, pretty things.* Is that small enough?

Or let's try: *Look at all the tiny, pretty things.*

If you want it to be tiny like the end of a pencil, maybe it would have that kind of flow. But if you wanted to think about a bunch of little flowers, you might want to put *little* instead of *tiny*.

Or maybe you want us to look at a petal on a flower, and that's what you want us to see.

Each one of those words holds a certain amount of weight and value for a variety of reasons: sound, sight, what the author is intending at that time.

That editing and consideration is the difference between "Oh, yeah, I can see it ... it's kind of small" and really thinking about the relationship the reader has with the words when they hear them in their head. *How* small do you want them to perceive this thing?

Where we break the line matters. *Look / At the little, tiny things* is different than *Look at / The little, tiny things*. Look at what? You have to wait till the next line!

And this is not magic. This is technique. A lot of times people are averse to editing. We've been taught that editing is unromantic, uncool. But to me, that's where the flowering comes through.

Tracie Morris won a 2021 Guggenheim Fellowship. Her most recent book is Who Do with Words [2018].

ESSAY & MEMOIR

The Writers' Workshop is far from the only game in literary Iowa City. Just across the street from Dey House sits the new, modernist HQ of the university's acclaimed Nonfiction Writing Program. Ambitions run just as high among the essayists, memoirists and journalists. "The aspiration is really expanding the whole notion of what an essay can be," says Inara Verzemnieks, MFA graduate, now assistant professor. A former newspaper reporter and Pulitzer finalist, Verzemnieks authored *Among the Living and the Dead*, a fusion of personal memoir, family story and world history. She says that a program with a rich legacy encourages that stretch—as does Iowa's relative modesty. "You feel like you're working off the map, in a sense, in a place where experiment is welcome." Sources of inspiration:

CLASSICS

PLUTARCH'S PARALLEL LIVES

Straight from the second century, the original celebrity profiles.

ZORA NEALE HURSTON

The novelist hit home in essay mode: funny, combative.

JOHN HERSEY'S HIROSHIMA

Epic reconstruction traces the atom bomb's repercussions.

IOWA CONNECTIONS

EULA BISS' HAVING AND BEING HAD

Program grad's 2020 meditation on consumer life.

KERRY HOWLEY

New York feature ace bridges straight reporting, genre-busting.

JOHN D'AGATA'S LIFESPAN OF A FACT

Collab with fact-checker Jim Fingal examines truth, how we know.

D'Agata, a Nonfiction Program professor, edited the anthology The Next American Essay.

PLAYWRITING

On the class list for the Iowa Playwrights Workshop:

Workshop / Playwriting: Fundamentals for Experts / Writing for Film / Classical to Romantic Theatre / Modern Drama / Post-Modern Theatre / Directing [or] Dramaturgy / History [and/or] Literature [x2] / Thesis: Full-Length Play

BOOKS ABOUT WRITING

THE WRITING LIFE by Annie Dillard 1989. Head-on, poetic advice: "The line of words is a miner's pick, a woodcarver's gouge, a surgeon's probe."

WORKING by Robert Caro 2019. The legendary biographer walks us through his immersive, slow-burn reporting technique.

CRAFT IN THE REAL WORLD by Matthew Salesses 2021. No-holds-barred takedown of workshop tradition, weaving many cultures' literary modes into a critique of U.S. expectations.

ON WRITING by Eudora Welty 2002. Elegant analysis from the 1977 Pulitzer winner.

A POETRY HANDBOOK by Mary Oliver 1994. The late poet writes, "Good poems are the best teachers." But she turns out to be a great one too.

HOW FICTION WORKS by James Wood 2008. A brainy, careful survey of storytelling tactics.

MY TRADE IS MYSTERY by Carl Phillips 2022. A poet's brief but incisive thoughts on necessary qualities: ambition, practice, community, stamina.

WRITING DOWN THE BONES by Natalie Goldberg 1986. Short chapters, practical exercises: rules to write by, from a Zen perspective.

ELEMENTS OF STYLE by Strunk & White 1959. Midcentury American monument: E.B. White's remake of William Strunk's basics guide. Grab Maira Kalman's illustrated edition.

MEANDER, SPIRAL, EXPLODE by Jane Alison 2019. A novelist explores different ways to "see" story structure. Fascinating and twisty in itself.

NOVELIST AS A VOCATION by Haruki Murakami 2022. Few will get a chance to crack a cold beer with the Japanese icon. This is next-best.

DREYER'S ENGLISH by Benjamin Dreyer 2019. Down with wan intensifiers! Random House's copy chief hands down a punchy style manifesto.

BIRD BY BIRD by Anne Lamott 1994. Funny, chatty, with the most accurate thing said about first drafts. Companion on many a misadventure.

Online, find science fiction writer N.K. Jemisin's insight on inventing fictional worlds.

PRAIRIE LIGHTS

A famed bookstore's signature events.

Unassuming when spied from across Dubuque Street in downtown Iowa City, the bookstore Prairie Lights holds down an outsize place in literary America. Given Iowa City's concentration of writers and readers, the four-decade-old shop has become a coveted stop for touring authors. Indeed, if what you most wanted in life was to see America's writers live, stationing yourself here would do the trick. Under the banner **LIVE FROM PRAIRIE LIGHTS**, the store stacks the calendar with readings and "in conversation" nights. Digitally streamed, archived in various online places, they're worth digging for: a unique record of modern American literary culture. [Seek out the Bernie Sanders, Susan Sontag and Norman Mailer sessions.] While some big-name draws move to the Englert Theatre, most of the readings take place in Prairie Lights' cozy confines, an intimate parlor of words, thought and community. *prairielights.com*

HOMEGOING
a novel
YAA GYASI
EDINBURGH
ALEXANDER CHEE
Flannery O'Connor
EVERYTHING THAT RISES MUST CONVERGE
A BAD GIRL'S BOOK OF ANIMALS
WONGMAY
A Home at the End of the World
Michael Cunningham
Drinking Coffee Elsewhere
ZZ PACKER

PERSPECTIVES

"As soon as you arrive in Iowa City, you realize that this is a place that takes its literary heritage very seriously. People are as proud of the Writers' Workshop as they are of the Hawkeyes. It's a place where it doesn't feel unreasonable to call yourself a writer, which is the first step toward becoming one. Most of us were spending our time writing, doing some teaching, and just hanging out with each other. Reading the same books, thinking about the same problems, arguing about similes until 2 a.m. over $4 pitchers of beer at the Fox Head. I've never had such a pure relationship with the craft at any other time."
—**LILA BYOCK**, television writer, *Watchmen*, *Manhattan*, etc.

"The sky is so vast, so big, that your mind kind of opens up. Your gaze travels. My first year here, in the springtime, I was out on my bike and with a cycling group. You could almost see the clouds dancing in front of you. You just sit there and watch these enormous patterns and shapes come out of the sky. And the guy next to me said, 'This is why we're in Iowa.' In the workshop, it's cool how radically different the work is. You feel like you're entering a totally different mind. There are so many works that are almost uncategorizable: you can't put them into a genre, you can't put them into a shape, but you're able to see their own logic. They're building their own system in front of you."
—**RAEDEN RICHARDSON**, 2022 Writers' Workshop MFA graduate

"A collision of occurrences made Iowa City a great place for creative practice. One of the most important moments was in 1922, when Carl Seashore, the dean of the graduate college at the University of Iowa, decided to allow creative work to be accepted as theses for advanced degrees. That began the process of inviting artists here to work and teach, and started this incredibly fertile feedback loop. It's really interesting that an academic policy decision can shape a place and its culture, but when you think about it, this is how you end up with a Kurt Vonnegut living on the North Side of Iowa City. People come here to learn and teach creative practice, and that inevitably filters out to the wider community of the town and then the state. Is it perfect? No. But the university and the broader community here respect creativity and foster it."
—**ANDRE PERRY**, author of *Some of Us Are Very Hungry Now*, executive director, Hancher Auditorium

INCLUDED

INTERVIEWS

Ten conversations with locals of note about writing books, writing plays, wrestling, farming, quilting, winning blue ribbons, building homes and selling T-shirts

ETHAN CANIN

AUTHOR

MY FOLKS ARE both from New York—Queens and Brooklyn, from the days when Brooklyn was really Brooklyn.

MY DAD'S A VIOLINIST. His first job, when he was 20 or something, was teaching violin at the University of Iowa.

I LIVED IN Iowa City till I was one or so. Where I live now is about 200 yards away. I've seen that house enough times, I can pretend I remember.

I WENT TO grad school at the Writers' Workshop. I went to medical school, became a doctor, all this stuff. We lived in South America for six months or so. We came back, living in San Francisco, and I was day-trading stocks.

THE UNIVERSITY of Iowa called and said, "Do you want a job? You want a tenured professorship?" I said, "No thank you."

I WAS 30 and didn't know what an incredible offer that was.

SO THEY SAID, "Well, how about coming out for a semester?"

I GOT A parking ticket on my first day. It was $3. I started thinking we could live here.

WE FELT LIKE someone was giving us two extra hours a day.

LITERARY WRITERS—it's a pretty obscure group to begin with. Who wants to be a literary writer? In Iowa City, they are heroes like no other place in the world.

IT IS THE best place that I've ever been for a literary writer. Way better than New York City, for example.

PEOPLE KNOW WHAT it is. The guy pumping your gas has an MFA in poetry.

BOOKS HAVE GOTTEN bigger, ambition has gotten bigger and more worldly. I could basically trace that to the internet. It's made research much easier. It's like a boost.

WHEN I FIRST started, if you wanted to write about Madagascar, you had to go to Madagascar.

FOR A WHILE, every single person in the United States was writing a postapocalyptic weather novel.

PEOPLE WHO FIND their way to my classes tend to write sort of character-based, longer work that basically deals with someone's life.

YOU'RE NEVER GOING to find another place where people are going to spend this much time reading your 20 pages.

GOING OVER EVERY word, because they care about it too.

HANNAH BRECKBILL

FARMER

WE HAVE 22 ACRES of vegetables. Late April, early May, we're able to start planting. We get everything going that can tolerate a little bit of frost.

OUR GREENS, our kale, Brussels sprouts, broccoli, carrots.

THEN THERE'S a big push in May, and by June, almost everything's in the ground.

WE'RE STILL planting successions of lettuce all through August.

WE HAVE SHEEP, mostly grazing rotationally. At the moment, they're in one section of the vegetable field. We're feeding them there all winter so they can deposit their fertility right there. They're multipurpose.

MY PARENTS WERE academics. I was a math major. Halfway through college, I was pretty sick of abstraction.

FOR THE FIRST four years of Humble Hands Harvest, I rented. I needed permanent land. I wanted to invest in trees and in the soil.

I ALSO WANTED someone to collaborate with, equally invested. Emily, my co-farmer, joined me, and we got ownership of a small piece of land.

THIS LAND HAD been a conventional cornfield on a dead-end road. The owners were selling, and the neighbors were worried about what would happen.

SO MY NEIGHBOR Steve organized about 20 people who put in money, formed an LLC and bought the land.

I HAD JUST enough money in my bank account to buy a share.

THERE'S A SENSE that farmers work hard. Absolutely true. But it's kind of a self-fulfilling prophecy.

ACTUALLY MY GOAL is not to work that hard. Farmers should have as much leisure time as anyone else should have.

ROD ZEITLER

BLUE-RIBBON WINNER

THE IOWA STATE FAIR has the largest food competition of any state fair. Hard to believe.

TEXAS STATE FAIR is supposed to be the best. The Minnesota State Fair is supposed to be the best. But we have more food categories and entries than they do.

THERE ARE DIVISIONS, and then classes, okay? The divisions are pickles or jams.

WITHIN PICKLES, there are 30-some different classes.

THERE ARE SWEET pickles, sliced horizontal. There are kosher dills. There are watermelon rind pickles.

KOSHER DILLS ARE really quick. You just take a whole cucumber, you put garlic in with it and the appropriate amount of salt and vinegar, and you're done.

WHEREAS, LET'S SAY, bread-and-butter pickles, you have to slice them an eighth of an inch thick, you have to slice green peppers, you have to slice onions. You have to get a certain size of onion, because you don't want a big onion. Or, I don't.

MOST PEOPLE DON'T know me. I'll be standing there at the fair and people will be talking about, "Who is this guy, Zeitler?"

I'VE HAD PATIENTS of mine who've been up there, and they're saying, "Oh, he's my doctor."

I'M AN INTERNIST, working with adults. I just retired in June. I hadn't quite turned 70, but damn close.

IT WAS A good time to retire. I had all of June and July to work on stuff, which is good, because that's a busy time.

MY THING IS, I'm a quantity guy. I want to get something in every category if I can. Other people will focus their efforts, but not have as many entries.

I HAVE STIFF competition. I don't win everything.

AKWI NJI

ARTIST, WRITER, SCHOOL ADMINISTRATOR

THERE'S A PERCEPTION that Iowa is bland. Of all the muffins of the world, we're the bran muffin. Of all the ice cream, we're French vanilla. Or maybe not even *French* vanilla.

TO SOME DEGREE, it's wise to be the best-kept secret.

BUT WHEN PEOPLE from California, New York or Georgia say, "Really, what's there to do in Iowa?" I do perk up a little bit.

I BRISTLE UP a little bit. "Well, actually ..."

IT'S IMPORTANT AS an Iowan to be ever-vigilant about recognizing incredible diversity in our history.

IT'S ABOUT PRIDE in who we are and who we've been.

I WORK IN the Waterloo schools. The district is predominantly of color. The mayor, the police chief—they're Black. The community itself is relatively evangelical and blue collar. You look at it and think, *How does this all work together?*

I WAS BORN in Iowa City. Very soon, we went to Cameroon, where my dad was from. We lived there until I was about eight years old.

MY MOM and younger sister and I came back to Springville, and I've pretty much lived in Iowa ever since.

MY GRANDPA WAS a farmer and owned a hydraulics business. There was just this wonderful sense of family at this really old two-story farmhouse there in Springville.

WE'D ORDER PIZZA from Casey's and sit around watching the Disney Sunday night movie.

MY GRANDMOTHER grew up speaking Czech, so that was in our daily lives, too, in terms of the food she'd cook and how she'd scold us.

I WAS CERTAIN I'd find treasure out in the barns. I never did.

MARY FONS

QUILTER

IT'S A DEMOCRATIC art. You can be poor. You can be educated. You can be uneducated. You can be rich. You don't *have* to be anything.

MY MOM, Marianne Fons, started making quilts in Winterset around 1976, so I'm a second-generation quilt-maker.

MY MOM DECIDED to make a quilt, but didn't know how. She took a class, and there she met a person named Liz Porter.

THEY LEARNED TO make a quilt and started teaching together. They both had English degrees, so they wrote a book. I'm in it, actually: a very small child in a quilted vest, sitting on a hay rack.

THEN THEY WROTE another one. Fons and Porter became this powerhouse quilt duo. They started teaching on public TV, filmed right there in Des Moines, on a show they called *Love of Quilting*.

FROM A LITTLE TOWN in Iowa, my mom and Liz made a world.

I GREW UP in this quilt world that was growing all the time.

WHEN I WAS 28, my life fell apart. I had a very brief marriage, and I got really sick.

I STARTED MAKING quilts. It's ancient, this needle-in, needle-out thing.

I GOT ON the show with my mom. I was the beginner. Everything I learned how to do, I learned in the television studio.

I BECAME EDITOR of *Quiltfolk* magazine in 2017. I've left the editorship, but I'm doing different things for *Quiltfolk* now.

QUILT HISTORY IS the history of this country. It is a history of women. You learn everything you want to know about the good, bad and ugly in this country. Cotton and everything.

AND THERE'S THIS whole wonderful universe of quilts. I just haven't left, because I keep finding things that I love.

DEBORAH YARCHUN

PLAYWRIGHT

PLAYWRITING IS more communal than other kinds of writing.

YOU'RE SITTING IN an audience. If they're laughing at your joke, you feel less alone.

YOU CAN WATCH people physically lean forward and respond to the work.

I FELT IT in my body on a different level than anything else.

I HAD BEEN in a New York City whirl. A desperate need for time and space. The Iowa Playwrights Workshop was on my radar.

I LIKED THE variety of voices coming out of that program. I didn't get a sense that they had a specific aesthetic.

YOU WEREN'T GOING to suddenly come out a different writer, but you were going to develop your voice.

YOU HAVE TO write a full-length play every semester. You don't overthink your work.

THE WORKSHOP ISN'T a free-for-all. There's a structure.

WE START WITH "pops": What popped for you? What did you respond to immediately?

A PLAY IS a blueprint. It's not until it's embodied by actors that you understand how it works. It doesn't become fully formed until it's in front of an audience.

THE MORE CHANCES you have to be in the room with those collaborators, the better you get at doing it.

I WOULD FLY in and out of Chicago and pass Iowa 80, the world's largest truck stop. When I was working on *Drive*, a play about truck drivers losing their jobs to self-driving trucks, I decided to set it in Iowa.

A LOT OF my plays focus on intimate stories about isolated people. And there's something about Iowa: It's spread out, but there's also a real sense of community within it. It was the right fit.

CLARISSA CHUN

WRESTLING COACH

I DON'T REALLY expect to be recognized by random people.

BUT HERE, I'll be in the store and someone will say, "Hey Coach! Good luck!"

IN IOWA, every child knows wrestling.

I'M FROM HAWAI'I, and I'm trying to think if there's something there even remotely close. You would think surfing. But even surfing in Hawai'i is not to the level of wrestling in Iowa.

IT'S ROCKING. It is rocking. Oh my gosh. And the fans are educated. They clap for the littlest thing, a move that doesn't even score points.

AND IF IT'S a little closer than they want, or an upset, then it's tough. It's harsh, it's critical.

IT GETS COLD here. Wrestling's an indoor sport. Iowa has lots of farms, and farmers are hardworking people. I think it all goes hand in hand.

IT DOESN'T COST a lot to just go out there and put your hands on somebody.

STARTING A PROGRAM, you've got to get the culture right. Set the tone for the group, build a strong foundation.

THE STANDARD of excellence: how we're going to represent the University of Iowa women's wrestling team.

WHAT'S BEST FOR an individual might not be best for the program. I tell every recruit that not one person is going to be bigger than the program.

I'VE LOST GREAT potential recruits because of that. But I didn't lose sleep over it.

YES, THEY STEP OUT onto the mat against their opponent alone. But they have their team behind them, cheering for them, coaching them, hyping them up.

THAT ENERGY. They feed off each other.

MIKE DRAPER

FOUNDER, RAYGUN

HUMOR IN IOWA is much deeper than corn and pig jokes. This is the state that produced Johnny Carson. We took the Iowa humor that already existed and put it on a T-shirt.

WE OFTEN SAY the store is essentially what the internet would be if it came to life.

I WAS BORN at Lutheran Hospital in Des Moines. I'm sitting six blocks away from where I was born right now.

MY great-grandfather was the banker for Hy-Vee, the grocery chain. It's the most Iowa thing to look at this billions-of-dollars corporation and say, "Yeah, my great-grandpa was your founder's banker."

MY SENIOR YEAR at the University of Pennsylvania, I got rejected for a fellowship in the UK, which was a surprise. I had done no other planning for my future.

A FRIEND SUGGESTED that we start selling T-shirts on campus. Why not? I don't have anything else going on.

I ENJOYED IT! Yeah, this is what I'm going to do: sell T-shirts.

SOMEONE SUGGESTED that I go back to Des Moines and open a store on the east side.

I MOVED BACK in with my parents. My mom had left up all my Rage Against the Machine posters. A smooth transition into my old bunk bed.

FOR THE FIRST two years, I was the only employee. Rang up every sale. Printed every shirt. Designed every shirt. Opened the store. Closed the store. Unclogged the toilet.

DES MOINES: It's 500,000 people. I grew up there. I knew all the inside jokes. This would be our thing: ultra-positive slogans about Des Moines.

"IOWA: Wave next time you fly over." "Des Moines: Let us exceed your low expectations."

IT'S NOT LIKE we *just* learned that people call this "flyover country." Is the joke on us, or is the joke on people who think all you can do is fly over?

NOBODY GROWS UP in the Midwest thinking that they're the center of attention for the country.

EVEN IF YOU'RE in Chicago, you're always going to be slightly removed. And that's the voice you need to speak from.

I'M PROUD THAT this has become a place that someone can bring a visitor from out of town with the knowledge that this store is demonstrably better than whatever they have in their city. Unless that city also has a Raygun.

IT'S BEEN LIKE a hard-working indie band. A slow and steady march. We opened Iowa City in 2009. Kansas City in 2014. I think Chicago in 2019, Omaha in '20. Yeah, I don't know. There's no real secret to it. It's just putting in the time, I suppose.

WHEN YOUR REGION is a pioneer in industry, and then in industrial agriculture, and then you reach a point where those models aren't quite tenable, what you do is going to dictate what other places do in the future.

THERE'S A MIXTURE of meme culture becoming more important and all things local becoming more important.

IT USED TO be that having a Versace bag was a signal that you'd been to a city where Versace is sold. Now it just means you have an internet connection.

BUT YOU'RE NOT going to get a Des Moines shirt just anywhere. It means you're from here. You know this place.

I DO THIS job well: the job of humorous shopkeeper.

I THINK THE STORE demonstrates the complexity of the state. Football meets nature meets progressive ideas meets cat jokes.

ZACH MANNHEIMER

HOMEBUILDER

THERE WERE more than enough theater people in New York and Brooklyn. I did a trip to 22 cities, and I chose Des Moines.

I WANTED A CITY as close to 50/50 politically as I could find. A city that struggled to attract young people. Where the downtown needed to be revitalized.

WE FORMED A social club that became the cultural and educational center downtown—that ran for a little over 10 years. We renovated an old firehouse and did thousands of shows in all the arts disciplines.

WE DIDN'T KNOW it at the time, but we were doing economic development.

SMALLER TOWNS around the Midwest began calling us, saying, "Hey, we have empty buildings on Main Street. Can you help?"

ATLAS COMMUNITY STUDIOS has been running in various forms for about 10 years. We started off creating cultural centers and fun things: restaurants, breweries and coffee shops. And we still do that.

BUT HOUSING was the number one issue everywhere we went.

YOU CAN 3D-print the exterior walls of a house in 20 to 30 hours.

I GOT OBSESSED with it. I traveled the world to learn, and I started Alquist specifically to work on 3D-printed homes.

A 3D-PRINTED concrete home uses 50 percent less energy than a stick-built home. There's 90 percent less waste on the job site. And we want to get away from concrete eventually—start using plant-based elements like hempcrete, and recycled glass and plastic.

WHAT I LOVE about Iowa is that there is incredible opportunity to explore ideas and dreams.

I MEAN, I studied theater, and now I run a construction company. It doesn't get too different than that.

JAN WEISSMILLER

BOOKSTORE OWNER

I WAS THE first full-time employee at Prairie Lights.

JIM OPENED the store in May 1978. I got my BA in December. I came into the store to get a book, the biography of Maud Gonne, Yeats' paramour. Someone had ordered it for me as a graduation present.

I TOLD JIM I was going to get a job at a restaurant and save up for MFA programs. And he said, "Oh, no—just work here."

I SAID I WOULDN'T be able to make enough money. He said, "Well, we'll have coffee ..." He talked me into it

WE WERE THE first place in Iowa City to carry *The New York Times*. People from all the university departments came in—the medical school, the law school, the history department—just to get *The New York Times*.

THE STORE then was 1,000 square feet. It's 11,000 square feet now.

WE JOKE about how many books have been written in the cafe.

WHEN YIYUN LI had young children, she wrote in our cafe for eight hours a day.

I GET UP at 7:30 in the morning and I read. My husband brings me coffee, and I read for three hours. I don't like to just sample things and then talk about them. I like to read everything I can.

YOU MIGHT THINK that Prairie Lights wouldn't be stressed about having to have the big TikTok books in stock, but that's not true.

ALL ABOUT LOVE by bell hooks—you constantly have to be sure you have that.

WE STILL HAVE all the same bookcases from when we moved to this location in 1983. We have carpeting. It's not all hardwood floors and ladders.

I BELIEVE IN books. We have lots of books. We have almost no stuffed animals.

INCLUDED

Essays and selected writing by noted voices from the Iowa Prairie

RAKING IT IN

Written by **CLAIRE LOMBARDO**

I ARRIVED IN IOWA CITY in 2015 in one of the worst ways, I'd argue, to arrive anywhere: scared, confused, and hauling an 813-page draft of a plotless novel I'd been secretly working on for several years. Wide-eyed and lost, on an infernally hot August day, I unloaded my meager belongings into the second-floor unit of a quaint little farmhouse on Burlington Street. I discovered shortly thereafter that my apartment was infested with iridescent flies of a type, I soon learned, typically drawn to dead bodies.

"Probably something just died in your walls," my landlord—a kindly lifelong Iowan—said affably, and I willed myself to sleep that night, T-shirt wrapped protectively around my face, interpreting and reinterpreting that particular phrase. I did not have to look very hard to see any number of cosmic signs that my novel and I were supposed to hightail it back to Chicago.

The only sign that I was supposed to be there, in Iowa City, was my recent acceptance into the Iowa Writers' Workshop, which I was convinced had been a clerical error. The offer had come on the heels of the most massive upheaval I've ever experienced. I'd very unexpectedly lost my father, and less unexpectedly dropped out of a graduate program in social work. I was, as a result, carrying around a great deal of unresolved emotional detritus and an impressive bundle of student loan debt. I was less a candidate for a prestigious writing program than for some kind of life-makeover ayahuasca retreat. Nevertheless, accident or no, the Writers' Workshop called, and when the Writers' Workshop calls, you answer.

For a writer, Iowa City is the mecca. One can't go anywhere in this town without tripping over a literary landmark: Mercy Hospital, which inspired Denis Johnson's "Emergency"; or St. Mary's Church, where

Flannery O'Connor reportedly prayed twice daily; or a bookishly named pet [I recently passed a sign for a missing cat named Rilke]; or—lo!—an *actual writer*, prone as writers are to ruminative meandering and/or procrastinatory trips to the Co-op. Thanks to the Writers' Workshop, the first and still most prominent creative-writing master of fine arts program in the world, shadows of John Cheever and Sandra Cisneros and Rita Dove are cast on every flat surface of Iowa City. Every single shadow, in turn, has a piece of dubious lore attached.

"That," a bartender once said, nodding as I sat down, "was Kurt Vonnegut's seat."

"You're in the Writers' Workshop?" someone asked me, making conversation in a high school auditorium during the Iowa caucuses, adding pleasantly, "My dad cheated on my mom with someone from the Writers' Workshop!"

I'm accustomed to these things now, more or less, having lived here for the better part of a decade, but when I arrived I couldn't get over them. There's a near-universal reverence in Iowa City for the writing arts, as well as an astronomical per-capita population of people who write. Joining these ranks exacerbated my anxiety tenfold. The panic attack I almost had, on my first day of classes, was not, then, entirely unexpected. Sitting in the close classroom on the second floor of Dey House, I felt sure that I was not only going to die but be remembered, forever, as the one who couldn't cut it, who lasted all of four minutes at the Writers' Workshop before, like an afflicted Dickensian urchin, she succumbed to a fatal attack of the vapors.

I wasn't supposed to be there. That was my conviction. I was not a *real writer* and not meant to spend my days among those who could reasonably call themselves such. Prior to moving to Iowa, I'd planned on being a therapist. I hadn't read most of the Books You're Supposed to Have Read; my writing life had consisted of secreted-away stories, moments stolen on the subway, jabbing furiously at the keyboard in my phone, or stray sentences spit out in the few seconds I looked away during my nightmarish nannying gig. I'd written a whole novel that way, in those off-hours. But I was the only one who had read it, and I had no idea whether it was viable. Whatever propelled the writers of Iowa City, decade after decade—I was sure I didn't have it.

Yet as a student in the Workshop, I'd been given enough money to pay my rent, and the permission to do nothing but write. And I knew what an enormous gift that is, the greatest and most alarming gift a writer can receive. And I knew I had to seize it, or at least try to, even though I wasn't entirely sure how.

I began, slowly, to ease my way in. The great pleasure of reading fiction, for me, is the permission to be elsewhere, and to dwell there deeply, and I—raw, new, very uncertain—needed that kind of buffer when I arrived in Iowa. So I read, and I wrote. On Halloween I walked home late through College Green Park, the moon an eerie purple overhead, then spent the evening with Shirley Jackson's *Hangsaman*. During the day, I migrated from one coffee shop in town to the next, dodging Iowa City's undergraduate masses and accompanied by James Baldwin, Grace Paley, Alice Munro. Wallace Stegner's *Crossing to Safety* kept me company on my front porch for a lovely string of warm fall evenings. And this proved my saving grace: the way I slowly retaught myself how to be a person in the world and how to be *a writer*, which, for me, simply meant that I wrote, constantly, when I wasn't reading.

Being at the Writers' Workshop is like being surrounded, every day, by a hundred versions of the most confusing person you've ever met. It is a hotbed for baffling, brilliant brains, egos that are at once enormous and eggshell-fragile, laundry lists of eccentricities both personal and vocational. It took me a while to see this place as my day-to-day reality instead of the lore that had preceded it, as my life instead of a mythology. I found a community, though, once I convinced myself nobody was going to revoke my acceptance. And I found in my classmates a great deal of wild intelligence and, often, just as much if not more compassion. I began to find friends, a mentor, a routine, and it was that way—reading and writing my way through—that I began to cobble together my writing life. The common denominator among myself and writers who'd preceded me at the Workshop, intimidating as I still found them—still *do* find them—was that we'd all, at some point, put our heads down and our pens to paper, and *written*.

I graduated from Iowa the June I was 28. That December, I finally finished my novel, *The Most Fun We Ever Had*, and my agent sent it off to publishers for consideration. I didn't know what to expect; what I one thousand percent did not expect was that nine of the 20 publishers would want to buy it. Or that I would just be sitting alone in my apartment on Burlington Street, like any other Thursday, while they competitively bid on the book from New York.

First, I puttered. I cleaned out my car, reorganized my kitchen cabinets, installed, with a hair dryer, winterizing plastic on my drafty windows. When not one of these tasks took as much time as I needed it to take, I called on novelist Ethan Canin, in whose classroom I had, more than two years earlier, nearly suffered a panic attack. Ethan had read my entire novel—that 813-page mess of a draft—and met with me every few weeks for a full year to give me notes. I will always consider myself invaluably lucky to have found a mentor in him, someone all too happy to share his abundant writerly knowledge, someone who supported his students wholeheartedly.

I told him about the auction, the winterizing plastic. "Come on over," he said.

This brand of kindness is not native to Iowa, nor specific to Iowa, but I have encountered it in Iowa more often than anywhere else.

"Put me to work," I told Ethan when I arrived, and so I was raking leaves from his front lawn the next time my agent called me with an update, much less anxious than I'd been that morning.

My focus, along with Ethan's repeated assurance that the interested parties in New York would not suddenly change their minds about wanting to buy my book, saw me through the rest of the afternoon. I attacked the Canins' lawn with vigor, moving piles of leaves onto a plastic tarp and then starting from the top, getting at them layer by layer. Chipping away, sticking with it: the best any of us can do, as writers, as humans; the only recourse we have, usually.

My novel, too, was so much less unwieldy than it had been when I made my trek to Iowa City from Chicago. My book would find its home that evening with the editor I'd dreamed of working with, and I will spare you—in the name of all the ghosts of all the great writers lurking around Iowa City—the easily grabbed allusion that I, too, had found my home by then. But, well, I had, and so perhaps I won't spare you. Iowa City had improbably become a haven for me, the best place in the world for me to be at the particular time I arrived there. I don't know if it needed me—yet another lost young person with a too-long novel—but I needed it, very much.

Earnestness hasn't felt particularly faddish of late, but it is

nevertheless a significant facet of the way I see the world. Not much feels as earnest to me as the time I spent at the Writers' Workshop.

"This is either the best or the worst job for a perfectionist," Ethan remarked, watching me with my rake. "You know you can't get every single leaf, right?"

This is writing, in a nutshell: trying, knowing you could do so forever, but keeping at it anyway. Defiant, I kept raking.

CLAIRE LOMBARDO's first novel, *The Most Fun We Ever Had*, was an instant *New York Times* bestseller and has been translated into over a dozen languages. A second novel, *World of Fools*, is forthcoming in 2024 from Doubleday Books. She has taught fiction writing at the University of Iowa and Grinnell College. Born and raised outside of Chicago, she now lives in Iowa City.

PARKING FOR ADELAIDE ON TUESDAYS

Written by JOE BLAIR

THERE'S NOTHING WILD ABOUT IOWA, the most cultivated state in the Union. But wilderness isn't so easily tamed. It's persistent. Turn your back for a minute, and it gains the upper hand on you.

Take Oxford, for example. The grain elevator on the Rock Island Line, scales and conveyors rusting, long ago surrendered to the weeds and small trees that sprout up around the foundation and between the sidetracks. The Carter Ford dealership, which used to be right downtown on Augusta Avenue, has been closed for a generation. Across the street, the Oxford Hardware Store, where my wife Deb and I were both employed 30 years ago, partially collapsed when a tornado touched down. The fancy restaurant in town, Augusta, got big ideas about itself and moved to Iowa City, where it failed. The sign, painted in black and white, is still somewhat fresh on the brick facade, but the building is empty and collapsing in slow motion. As are most of the buildings on the once-august main street. The Alibi, a good place to go 30 years ago if you wanted to get your ass kicked, is gone. The Dawg House might still be in business. Hard to judge from the street. There are two or three antique shops, but one posts a sign that reads "By Appointment Only." Nobody comes downtown. There is no reason to come. There's no purpose behind it anymore.

Property, therefore, is inexpensive. A storefront with two rooms out back is for sale. They're asking $40,000. Locals are driving back and forth, from The Depot convenience store to front porch, in their golf carts. One waves at us. Another man shouts, "Don't set there too long," as he motions toward a gray stone building that looks like a ruined castle, "that thing might fall on ya!" I laugh and shout back, "It looks like it might!" American Legion Post 541 is nothing more than a pole barn attached to a stick-framed trailer home, sheathed in particle board. Bingo on Fridays. The Sale Barn diner, where Deb and I, on break from the hardware store,

would eat a breakfast of two farm eggs with profoundly orange yolks and bacon and sourdough toast, still looks the same, painted white, pens and auction barn attached, the same sign out front: "Established in 1969." Another sign, a newer one at the head of an empty parking space, reads "Reserved Parking for Adelaide on Tuesdays." A man and a small boy fly a kite in the heartbreakingly humble park on the floodplain of Rhine Creek, and the whole world, the wind, the traffic out by the campgrounds on Route 80, sounds like waves, as Tom Petty puts it, crashing on the beach. What's left of Iowa's fabled tallgrass prairie can now be found in the 50-foot strips of wilderness that border the otherwise orderly fields of corn and beans. The vegetation that grows within the margins of the buffer strips—crabgrass, thistle, prairie grass, wildflowers and sumac—serves the purpose of reducing soil loss and providing habitat for pheasant, rabbits and redwing blackbirds. It also serves the purpose of being beautiful, blossoming in spring, and fading to tawny brown in winter.

Mike and I are moving again. It's what Mike wants. "Go somewhere, please," is his favorite sentence. Mike's autistic; he repeats this phrase over and over. And since he's asking so politely, I continue to drive. Between the two strips of wilderness, all the way to Mount Vernon.

Why Mount Vernon? Why not North Liberty or Burlington or Marshalltown or Dubuque? I don't know. There's no obvious destination here in Iowa. We don't have a shoreline. Or a major city with the attendant major art museums and airports. What we have are small clusters of electric lights you can spot on clear nights as you fly over. See that? That cluster is Dubuque. See the moon glancing off the Mississippi? And I think that one is Iowa City. And that little one up north might be Mount Vernon.

Fuel is a coffee shop that sells homemade cookies. "Do you want a cookie, Mike?" I say. "Do you want a cookie? Yes?" Mike doesn't answer. Apparently he's tired of saying words now. "Okay," I say. "We're going in. Do you want to go in?" Mike reaches to remove his seatbelt.

Mount Vernon has everything a small Midwestern town should have: A water tower. A park with a bandstand. A tiny cinderblock movie theater painted blue. A mom-and-pop grocery store. A bar. Another bar. Another bar. A diner. A restaurant. A pizza palace. A store that sells little plastic pigs capable of blowing pink bubbles out their asses when you squeeze them. An Ayurvedic apothecary. A century-old high school with a modest football stadium that is carved into the side of a hill. A hill. An antique shop.

Another bar. Another antique shop. A college. An Ace hardware store. And Fuel.

Fuel is the soul of the town. It sells cookies, like I said. It also sells hep-cat jewelry, and a white ceramic bust of a bald woman whose skull is divided up into the various zones of phrenological study, and a tiny wooden Ferris wheel peopled with intricately painted plastic figurines of dead presidents, and of course coffee. It is owned by Tommie, formerly of Minneapolis. Deb and I met Tommie twenty-some years ago during a Richard Thompson concert at the intersection of Iowa Avenue and Dubuque Street in Iowa City. Tommie has two children, Matisse and Beckett. Her mother's name is Pat. Pat's the one who bakes the cookies. I order one molasses and one snickerdoodle. I need to repeat this order due to my mask and the Plexiglass barricade between myself and the cashier. I notice Pat, moving between oven and refrigerator.

"Hi, Pat!" I shout.

Pat stops, turns, and squints in my direction.

"Who is that?" she says.

I'm holding Mike by the hand when she pushes aside the Covid barricade and steps out for a visit. I offer a fist bump. She does not accept it. "I've had my shots," she says.

"Me too," I say.

She steps close and we exchange a hug.

"Are you okay?" I say.

"I'm okay," she says.

"Pat," I say. "I just want to be honest. I think you need new glasses."

What I'm actually saying is, *I love you. I'm grateful that you're in the world. If it weren't for you and your cookies, I don't know if I'd be all that interested in continuing.*

"I do," she says, removing her glasses and looking at them. "These ones are all scratched up." What she's actually saying is, *I do. These ones are all scratched up.*

The air is dry and cool. The sky is the deep-blue color that only comes in spring and fall. Lilacs are in full bloom. On the way out of town, I wave to a chef I know who is also a musician and is just now opening the door to his car. He waves back. Mike and I take a left from 1st Street down the hill and past the old football field. I eat my snickerdoodle and take a left and drive south again. To the next town. Which, I've decided, will be West Branch,

CAFE
CAFE

birthplace of Herbert Hoover. Mike doesn't finish his molasses cookie. He holds it for a few miles, maybe out of courtesy, until he finally places it on the dash. So I eat that one too.

We bisect the neatly combed hills on Route 1, then east on 80. In West Branch, on North Downey Street where we finally park, the curb is almost two feet high, which makes it an easy place to sit. So that's where we do sit. We tried the bench across the street near the entrance to Herb N' Lou's, but that was in the shade, and we were a little chilly. Now we're in direct sunlight. We've brought our plastic cups of water with us, and they're resting beside us on the high concrete sidewalk. The cups are sweating profusely. There's sand on the surface of the sidewalk. One ant charges east and then west and then east again, following a chemical trail invisible to us. Mike leans his forearms on his thighs, his weight forward. He's frowning intently, partly because of the bright sunlight and partly because he frowns almost all the time, like he's trying hard to remember something.

There's a small museum here. Used to be curated by some historian or other who had written some Herbert Hoover book or other and who had taken what I'm sure he thought to be a plum gig at what he thought to be the apex of his career. When we met him at a museum open house, he was trying his best to get out of West Branch. He was a very sweet man. He tried to impress our children with his ability to stick his finger in his mouth and make that popping sound. I wish they would have pretended to be impressed. I really do. But they were not impressed, since I had already introduced them to the finger-in-mouth popping-noise thing. But Deb and I were in the market for a house at the time and we drove to his place. It was built from brick and it had granite details around the large windows.

Herbert Hoover and his wife, Lou, are buried in a clearing here at Herbert Hoover National Historic Site. This is the gravesite. And here is Herbert's 1874 house. This, his father's 1874 blacksmith shop. This, his old neighborhood, with its wooden walkways. Small vegetable garden, still tended. Shade trees. Mike and I have walked these paths many times. We've seen the trees mature from saplings to thick-wristed adults. We've visited the Herbert Hoover museum twice. Or maybe three times. There's a replica of a one-room schoolhouse there. A potbellied stove. The leading edges of the wooden desktops are rounded from the forearms and hands of students that have been dead for many years. The last time we visited the museum, fifteen years ago or so, was during the holidays. They had a Christmas tree exhibit. With decorations and lights and so forth. Some lukewarm hot chocolate. Music and so forth. And so on. It was depressing. But we love this gravesite. These two rectangular stones. This American flag, in every season. We love to tour the little park. We love the bar, Herb N' Lou's, which serves pizza.

That's what Mike and I are waiting for now, sitting in the spring sunshine on the curb in front of what was once a state bank. They haven't torn down the old downtown brick-and-granite row buildings yet. You can imagine the way it was—the bank here, hardware store there, clothing store, shoe store, haberdasher, dry goods store, Masonic hall, bakery.

Now, left to right, it's a building for lease, then Herb N' Lou's bar, then another building for lease, then Grandma's Knick Knack, the dog grooming place, Shear Creations, the tattoo and body piercing place, a museum, For Lease, For Lease, the ice cream parlor.

A line of elementary school children are on a field trip. They seem pretty happy. They're walking down the hill toward the ice cream parlor. No. Walking isn't the right word. They aren't walking. They're jumping and running and dancing and spinning along. I'm thinking it must be a special thing Mrs. Beckett allows every spring. Or Mr. McGovern. Or Miss Osterhaus. Every spring, Miss Osterhaus takes the kids on a field trip for ice cream.

Mike and I are sitting in the sunshine. A large red propane truck drives by. The driver waves at us. A white Chevy pickup truck drives by. The driver waves at us. Eventually, we must leave our historic spot on the historically high concrete sidewalk in front of what was once the State Bank and enter the one-time hardware store, where the pizza is almost ready.

We will sit by the front window. And an old guy, tall and broad-shouldered, while paying for his pizza and then leaving a tip in the jar, will drop his cane and cuss beneath his breath. I will move to stand, but I'll think twice. I won't want to insult him by offering to pick it up for him. But another guy, young, at another table will say, "I'll get that for you," and he'll spring to his feet and fetch the old man's cane. And the old man, who will be wearing a Yankees cap, will thank him and say, "I can get down okay But I can't get up so easy anymore. Not with this knee . . ." And when the old man turns to leave, he'll look directly at me and nod. And I, who will still be wearing my Red Sox cap, will say, pointing at my cap, "I would've gotten your cane if you weren't wearing that hat," and, unable to hear me, he will smile and say, "Yeah," and he'll step closer. "I got the other one done up in Minnesota, but now this one's bone-on-bone. That's what they say. But I'm eighty-seven years old." "You don't want anyone cutting you open," I'll say. "Well, I'm eighty-seven," he'll say. "Well," I'll say. And then I'll say something stupid like, "I'm doing my best to get there too," and he'll smile and say, "Well, have a good day. I'll see you later." And I'll say, "I'll see you later."

But I won't. I won't see him later. Mike will frown and lean forward and look out the front window of the old bar, which is named after the old president and his old wife. When the pizza's ready, I'll offer him a slice, but he won't be interested. It's not only words he has lost interest in. He's lost interest in food too. Soon we'll walk to the car. I'll carry the pizza box. And we'll pause to watch a second line of children spinning and running and jumping and dancing down the hill toward the ice cream shop.

It's the things that repeat themselves we'll miss. The other things, those exciting one-offs we thought we wanted so badly—those trips to the coast, the things we thought might break the tedium, the things that cost us so much, in dollars and arguments and marital spats—those things we won't even remember. It's the same curved surface we run our hand over again and again. This shape. This shape. This same small cluster of lights. This is what we'll remember. This is what we'll miss. If we can still miss anything, when we're gone from this place.

JOE BLAIR is a writer and refrigeration mechanic. He lives in Iowa.

SHOELESS JOE JACKSON COMES TO IOWA

Written by **W.P. KINSELLA**

Excerpted from chapter 1 of Shoeless Joe, *published* 1982.

My father said he saw him years later playing in a tenth-rate commercial league in a textile town in Carolina, wearing shoes and an assumed name.

"He'd put on fifty pounds and the spring was gone from his step in the outfield, but he could still hit. Oh, how that man could hit. No one has ever been able to hit like Shoeless Joe."

Three years ago at dusk on a spring evening, when the sky was a robin's-egg blue and the wind as soft as a day-old chick, I was sitting on the verandah of my farm home in eastern Iowa when a voice very clearly said to me, "If you build it, he will come."

The voice was that of a ballpark announcer. As he spoke, I instantly envisioned the finished product I knew I was being asked to conceive. I could see the dark, squarish speakers, like ancient sailors' hats, attached to aluminum-painted light standards that glowed down into a baseball field, my present position being directly behind home plate.

In reality, all anyone else could see out there in front of me was a tattered lawn of mostly dandelions and quack grass that petered out at the edge of a cornfield perhaps fifty yards from the house.

Anyone else was my wife Annie, my daughter Karin, a corn-colored collie named Carmeletia Pope, and a cinnamon and white guinea pig named Junior who ate spaghetti and sang each time the fridge door opened. Karin and the dog were not quite two years old.

"If you build it, he will come," the announcer repeated in scratchy Middle American, as if his voice had been recorded on an old 78-r.p.m. record.

A three-hour lecture or a 500-page guide book could not have given me clearer directions: dimensions of ballparks jumped over and around me like fleas, cost figures for light standards and floodlights whirled around my head like the moths that dusted against the porch light above me.

That was all the instruction I ever received: two announcements and a vision of a baseball field. I sat on the verandah until the satiny dark was complete. A few curdly clouds striped the moon, and it became so silent I could hear my eyes blink.

Our house is one of those massive old farm homes, square as a biscuit box with a sagging verandah on three sides. The floor of the verandah slopes so that marbles, baseballs, tennis balls, and ball bearings all accumulate in a corner like a herd of cattle clustered with their backs to a storm. On the north verandah is a wooden porch swing where Annie and I sit on humid August nights, sip lemonade from teary glasses, and dream.

THAT WAS ALL THE INSTRUCTION I EVER RECEIVED: TWO ANNOUNCEMENTS AND A VISION OF A BASEBALL FIELD. I SAT ON THE VERANDAH UNTIL THE SATINY DARK WAS COMPLETE.

When I finally went to bed, and after Annie inched into my arms in that way she has, like a cat that you suddenly find sound asleep in your lap, I told her about the voice and I told her that I knew what it wanted me to do. "Oh love," she said, "if it makes you happy you should do it," and she found my lips with hers. I shivered involuntarily as her tongue touched mine.

Annie: She has never once called me crazy. Just before I started the first landscape work, as I stood looking out at the lawn and the cornfield, wondering how it could look so different in daylight, considering the notion of accepting it all as a dream and abandoning it, Annie appeared at my side and her arm circled my waist. She leaned against me and looked up, cocking her head like one of the red squirrels that scamper along the power lines from the highway to the house. "Do it, love," she said as I looked down at her, that slip of a girl with hair the color of cayenne pepper and at least a million freckles on her face and arms, that girl who lives in blue jeans and T-shirts and at twenty-four could still pass for sixteen.

I thought back to when I first knew her. I came to Iowa to study.

She was the child of my landlady. I heard her one afternoon outside my window as she told her girl friends, "When I grow up I'm going to marry ... " and she named me. The others were going to be nurses, teachers, pilots, or movie stars, but Annie chose me as her occupation. Eight years later we were married. I chose willingly, lovingly, to stay in Iowa. Eventually I rented this farm, then bought it, operating it one inch from bankruptcy. I don't seem meant to farm, but I want to be close to this precious land, for Annie and me to be able to say, "This is ours."

Now I stand ready to cut into the cornfield, to chisel away a piece of our livelihood to use as dream currency, and Annie says, "Oh, love, if it makes you happy you should do it." I carry her words in the back of my mind, stored the way a maiden aunt might wrap a brooch, a remembrance of a long-lost love. I understand how hard that was for her to say and how it got harder as the project advanced. How she must have told her family not to ask me about the baseball field I was building, because they stared at me dumb-eyed, a row of silent, thickset peasants with red faces. Not an imagination among them except to forecast the wrath of God that will fall on the heads of pagans such as I.

"If you build it, he will come."

He, of course, was Shoeless Joe Jackson.

Joseph Jefferson [Shoeless Joe] Jackson
Born: Brandon Mills, South Carolina, July 16, 1887
Died: Greenville, South Carolina, December 5, 1951

In April 1945, Ty Cobb picked Shoeless Joe as the best left fielder of all time. A famous sportswriter once called Joe's glove "the place where triples go to die." He never learned to read or write. He created legends with a bat and a glove.

Was it really a voice I heard? Or was it perhaps something inside me making a statement that I did not hear with my ears but with my heart? Why should I want to follow this command? But as I ask, I already know the answer. I count the loves in my life: Annie, Karin, Iowa, Baseball. The great god Baseball.

My birthstone is a diamond. When asked, I say my astrological sign is "hit and run," which draws a lot of blank stares here in Iowa where 50,000 people go to see the University of Iowa Hawkeyes football team while 500 regulars, including me, watch the baseball team perform.

My father, I've been told, talked baseball statistics to my mother's belly while waiting for me to be born. My father: born, Glen Ullin, North Dakota, April 14, 1896. Another diamond birthstone. Never saw a professional baseball game until 1919 when he came back from World War I where he had been gassed at Passchendaele. He settled in Chicago, inhabited a room above a bar across from Comiskey Park, and quickly learned to live and die with the White Sox. Died a little when, as prohibitive favorites, they lost the 1919 World Series to Cincinnati, died a lot the next summer when eight members of the team were accused of throwing that World Series.

Before I knew what baseball was, I knew of Connie Mack, John McGraw, Grover Cleveland Alexander, Ty Cobb, Babe Ruth, Tris Speaker, Tinker-to-Evers-to-Chance, and, of course, Shoeless Joe Jackson. My father loved underdogs, cheered for the Brooklyn Dodgers and the hapless St. Louis Browns, loathed the Yankees—an inherited trait, I believe—and insisted that Shoeless Joe was innocent, a victim of big business and crooked gamblers.

That first night, immediately after the voice and the vision, I did nothing except sip my lemonade a little faster and rattle the ice cubes in my glass. The vision of the baseball park lingered—swimming, swaying, seeming to be made of red steam, though perhaps it was only the sunset. And there was a vision within the vision: one of Shoeless Joe Jackson playing left field. Shoeless Joe Jackson who last played major league baseball in 1920 and was suspended for life, along with seven of his compatriots, by Commissioner Kenesaw Mountain Landis, for his part in throwing the 1919 World Series.

Instead of nursery rhymes, I was raised on the story of the Black Sox Scandal, and instead of Tom Thumb or Rumpelstiltskin, I grew up hearing of the eight disgraced ballplayers: Weaver, Cicotte, Risberg, Felsch, Gandil, Williams, McMullin, and, always, Shoeless Joe Jackson.

"He hit .375 against the Reds in the 1919 World Series and played errorless ball," my father would say, scratching his head in wonder. "Twelve hits in an eight-game series. And *they* suspended *him*," Father

would cry. Shoeless Joe became a symbol of the tyranny of the powerful over the powerless. The name Kenesaw Mountain Landis became synonymous with the Devil.

Building a baseball field is more work than you might imagine. I laid out a whole field, but it was there in spirit only. It was really only left field that concerned me. Home plate was made from pieces of cracked two-by-four embedded in the earth. The pitcher's rubber rocked like a cradle when I stood on it. The bases were stray blocks of wood, unanchored. There was no backstop or grandstand, only one shaky bleacher beyond the left-field wall. There was a left-field wall, but only about fifty feet of it, twelve feet high, stained dark green and braced from the rear. And the left-field grass. My intuition told me that it was the grass that was important. It took me three seasons to hone that grass to its proper texture, to its proper color. I made trips to Minneapolis and one or two other cities where the stadiums still have natural-grass infields and outfields. I would arrive hours before a game and watch the groundskeepers groom the field like a prize animal, then stay after the game when in the cool of the night the same groundsmen appeared with hoses, hoes, and rakes, and patched the grasses like medics attending to wounded soldiers.

I pretended to be building a Little League ballfield and asked their secrets and sometimes was told. I took interest in the total operation; they wouldn't understand if I told them I was building only a left field.

Three seasons I've spent seeding, watering, fussing, praying, coddling that field like a sick child. Now it glows parrot-green, cool as mint, soft as moss, lying there like a cashmere blanket. I've begun watching it in the evenings, sitting on the rickety bleacher just beyond the fence. A bleacher I constructed for an audience of one.

My father played some baseball, Class B teams in Florida and California. I found his statistics in a dusty minor-league record book. In Florida he played for a team called the Angels and, according to his records, was a better-than-average catcher. He claimed to have visited all forty-eight states and every major-league ballpark before, at forty, he married and settled down in Montana, a two-day drive from the nearest major-league team. I tried to play, but ground balls bounced off my chest and fly balls dropped between my hands. I might have been a fair designated hitter, but the rule was too late in coming.

There is the story of the urchin who, tugging at Shoeless Joe

Jackson's sleeve as he emerged from a Chicago court-house, said, "Say it ain't so, Joe."

Jackson's reply reportedly was, "I'm afraid it is, kid."

When he comes, I won't put him on the spot by asking. The less said the better. It is likely that he did accept money from gamblers. But throw the Series? Never! Shoeless Joe Jackson led both teams in hitting in that 1919 Series. It was the circumstances. The circumstances. The players were paid peasant salaries while the owners became rich. The infamous Ten Day Clause, which voided contracts, could end any player's career without compensation, pension, or even a ticket home.

The second spring, on a toothachy May evening, a covering of black clouds lumbered off westward like ghosts of buffalo, and the sky became the cold color of a silver coin. The forecast was for frost.

The left-field grass was like green angora, soft as a baby's cheek. In my mind I could see it dull and crisp, bleached by frost, and my chest tightened.

But I used a trick a groundskeeper in Minneapolis had taught me, saying he learned it from grape farmers in California. I carried out a hose, and, making the spray so fine it was scarcely more than fog, I sprayed the soft, shaggy spring grass all that chilled night. My hands ached and my face became wet and cold, but, as I watched, the spray froze on the grass, enclosing each blade in a gossamer-crystal coating of ice. A covering that served like a coat of armor to dispel the real frost that was set like a weasel upon killing in the night. I seemed to stand taller than ever before as the sun rose, turning the ice to eye-dazzling droplets, each a prism, making the field an orgy of rainbows.

Annie and Karin were at breakfast when I came in, the bacon and coffee smells and their laughter pulling me like a magnet. "Did it work, love?" Annie asked, and I knew she knew by the look on my face that it had. And Karin, clapping her hands and complaining of how cold my face was when she kissed me, loved every second of it.

"And how did he get a name like Shoeless Joe?" I would ask my father, knowing the story full well but wanting to hear it again. And no matter how many times I heard it, I would still picture a lithe ballplayer, his great bare feet white as baseballs sinking into the outfield grass as he sprinted for a line drive. Then, after the catch, his toes gripping the grass like claws, he would brace and throw to the infield.

"It wasn't the least bit romantic," my dad would say. "When he was

still in the minor leagues he bought a new pair of spikes and they hurt his feet. About the sixth inning he took them off and played the outfield in just his socks. The other players kidded him, called him Shoeless Joe, and the name stuck for all time."

It was hard for me to imagine that a sore-footed young outfielder taking off his shoes one afternoon not long after the turn of the century could generate a legend.

I came to Iowa to study, one of the thousands of faceless students who pass through large universities, but I fell in love with the state. Fell in love with the land, the people, the sky, the cornfields, and Annie. Couldn't find work in my field, took what I could get. For years, I bathed each morning, frosted my cheeks with Aqua Velva, donned a three-piece suit and snap-brim hat, and, feeling like Superman emerging from a telephone booth, set forth to save the world from a lack of life insurance. I loathed the job so much that I did it quickly, urgently, almost violently. It was Annie who got me to rent the farm. It was Annie who got me to buy it. I operate it the way a child fits together his first puzzle, awkwardly, slowly, but, when a piece slips into the proper slot, with pride and relief and joy.

I built the field and waited, and waited, and waited.

"It will happen, honey," Annie would say when I stood shaking my head at my folly. People looked at me. I must have had a nickname in town. But I could feel the magic building like a gathering storm. It felt as if small animals were scurrying through my veins. I knew it was going to happen soon.

One night I watch Annie looking out the window. She is soft as a butterfly, Annie is, with an evil grin and a tongue that travels at the speed of light. Her jeans are painted to her body, and her pointy little nipples poke at the front of a black T-shirt that has the single word RAH! emblazoned in waspish yellow capitals. Her red hair is short and curly. She has the green eyes of a cat.

Annie understands, though it is me she understands and not always what is happening. She attends ballgames with me and squeezes my arm when there's a hit, but her heart isn't in it and she would just as soon be at home. She loses interest if the score isn't close, or the weather's not warm, or the pace isn't fast enough. To me it is baseball, and that is all that matters. It is the game that's important—the tension, the strategy, the ballet of the fielders, the angle of the bat.

"There's someone on your lawn," Annie says to me, staring out into the orange-tinted dusk. "I can't see him clearly, but I can tell someone is there." She was quite right, at least about it being *my* lawn, although it is not in the strictest sense of the word a lawn; it is a *left field.*

I have been more restless than usual this night. I have sensed the magic drawing closer, hovering somewhere out in the night like a zeppelin, silky and silent, floating like the moon until the time is right.

Annie peeks through the drapes. "There is a man out there, I can see his silhouette. He's wearing a baseball uniform, an old-fashioned one."

"It's Shoeless Joe Jackson," I say. My heart sounds like someone flicking a balloon with his index finger.

W.P. KINSELLA [1935-2016] was a Canadian novelist and short story writer and a graduate of the Iowa Writers' Workshop in 1978. Among several key subjects, much of his work revolves around baseball. *Shoeless Joe* became the basis for the film *Field of Dreams*.

THREE POEMS

Written by **JULIÁN DAVID BAÑUELOS**

THE DAY THE PELICANS ARRIVED IN IOWA

Ayer, we spoke of our different worlds
then wept together, hoy, I woke enraged,
what a terrible way to start the day
I know, but I think I figured it out:
Media Narnaja, this cruel world gathers
picks and chooses its victims upon birth.
Soy celoso because I have begged death
to return and to take the best of me

to return and take the best of others.
But this is how it was, not how it is.
Without you, without me, the world lacks love.
Some days end así: whirling of feathers
magnificent hues, and the cries of birds.
Let's watch as the world closes behind us.

"WHAT ELSE BESIDES BUDDY HOLLY?"

the Hub City feels like: night
torn roofer palms
held up 5 o' clock
shadow
where
narcan nasal spray
wakes Buddy Holly fanatics
& rattlesnakes rattle
tattle tales
tall as mulberry trees
gravel the knee
until a view
is just that
a view in the rear—
a viewing
a mirror can only give
where
bolls of cotton
become dirt
where the keys lay
under door mats
where the winds
swing open screen doors
on lay of the land
a whole lot

of nothing or something reined in
by the outstretched arms
of bodies
ready to wake.

for Reginald Dwayne Betts

CERTAINTY FORMED

Before I take hold of the sky's edges
I spy our prayers both brash and bold pierce
the high layered clouds. I shake the air, snow falls
and I exhale— the atmosphere crumbles
onto the farm road where I play connect
the dots, sketching asterisms with you—
Outstretched, winding, and identifying
we give names to things that feel out of reach.

Moving around inside me, down below—
the whir of sin mixes with kerosene.
Amor, what's left under the underpass
are flowering hymns and what's left of me
is windblown, afar, and collecting dust.
What's left of me is alive and blooming.

JULIÁN DAVID BAÑUELOS is a Chicano poet and translator from Lubbock, Texas. He is a graduate of the Iowa Writers' Workshop and lives and teaches in Iowa City.

DIRECTORY
& INDEX

DIRECTORY

BOOKSHOPS

Beaverdale Books *Des Moines*
Book People *Sioux City*
The Book Rack *Davenport*
The Book Shoppe *Boone*
Book Vault *Oskaloosa*
The Book Vine *Cherokee*
The BookWorm *Bellevue*
Brick Road Books *Winterset*
Burlington By the Book *Burlington*
The Curiosity Shop *Pella*
Dog-Eared Books *Ames*
Dragonfly Books *Decorah*
Green Dragon Bookshop *Fort Dodge*
The Haunted Bookshop *Iowa City*
Hedgie's *Bedford*
Next Page Books *Cedar Rapids*
Pageturners Bookstore *Indianola*
Pella Books *Pella*
Pioneer Bookshop *Grinnell*
Plain Talk *Des Moines*
Prairie Lights *Iowa City*
Raccoon River Press *West Des Moines*
Reading in Public *West Des Moines*
River Lights Bookstore *Dubuque*
Rivertown Fine Books *McGregor*
Shady Character Books *Cedar Rapids*
Sidekick Coffee & Books *Iowa City*
Soul Book Nook *Waterloo*
Storyhouse Bookpub *Des Moines*
Swamp Fox Bookstore *Marion*

BREWERIES

515 Brewing *Des Moines*
7 Hills Brewing *Dubuque*
Adventurous Brewing *Bettendorf*
Alluvial *Ames*
Barn Town *West Des Moines*
Big Grove *Solon, etc.*
Blind Butcher *Inwood*
Confluence Brewing *Des Moines*
Dimensional *Dubuque*
Fenceline Beer Lab *Huxley*
Fenders *Polk City*
Full Fledged *Council Bluffs*
Gezellig *Newton*
Iowa Brewing Co. *Cedar Rapids*
Jackson Street Brewing *Sioux City*
Kalona Brewing Co. *Kalona*
Lion Bridge *Cedar Rapids*
Lua Brewing *Des Moines*
Maquoketa Brewing *Maquoketa*
Mason City Brewing *Mason City*
The Old Man River *McGregor*
Peace Tree *Des Moines*
PIVO *Calmar*
Pulpit Rock *Decorah*
Reclaimed Rails *Bondurant*
SingleSpeed *Cedar Falls*
Toppling Goliath *Decorah*
Twin Span *Bettendorf*
Twisted Vine *Des Moines*
Wise I *Le Mars*

HARDWARE & FARM SUPPLY

Ankeny Hardware *Ankeny*
Boone Hardware *Boone*
Edgewood Farm & Home *Edgewood*
Elevator Farm Store *Wapello*
Farm & City Supply *Des Moines*
Fisk Farm & Home *Monona, Decorah, Cresco*
Fred's Feed & Supply LLC *West Liberty*
H&M Farm & Home *Sigourney*
Jewell Farm & Home *Jewell*
Knoxville Farm & Home *Knoxville*
McCorkle Farm & Home *Columbia*
Miller's Hardware *Des Moines*
Nelson Farm Supply *Harlan*
New Providence Hardware *New Providence*
Ogden Farm & Feed Center *Ogden*
Parkersburg Hardware *Parkersburg*
Welsh's Village Farm & Home *Lansing*
Wilmes Hardware *Sioux City*

INDEX